ECOLOGICAL PS
Volume 17, Numbe

SPECIAL IS
SYMMETRY AND DUALITY:
PRINCIPLES FOR AN ECOLOGICAL PSYCHOLOGY, I
Claudia Carello, Guest Editor

ECOLOGICAL PSYCHOLOGY, 17(3 & 4), 131–133

INTRODUCTION

Symmetry and Duality: Principles for an Ecological Psychology, I

Claudia Carello and M. T. Turvey

Center for the Ecological Study of Perception and Action
University of Connecticut

The paradox is now firmly established that the utmost abstractions are the weapons of control over thoughts of concrete fact. (Whitehead, 1925/1967, p. 32)

In June of 2004 a conference entitled Symmetry and Duality: Principles for an Ecological Psychology was held at the University of Connecticut in honor of Robert E. Shaw. Students, colleagues, and friends recounted Shaw's influence, whether explicit or implicit, on their thinking. Shaw's propensity for abstraction was recounted with amusement. Various incarnations of Bob's course, benignly named "Introduction to Cognitive Systems," introduced the audience (which typically included faculty and repeat auditors along with registered students) to the likes of metric tensors, Doxastic knowledge, functors, nonabelian gauge groups, and so on—in a style that evolved from the "vrooming" of the University of Minnesota years to the "wild ride" of today's Center for the Ecological Study of Perception and Action at the University of Connecticut. Shaw's propensity for abstraction was also recounted with admiration for the essence of the paradox identified by Whitehead (1925): The right abstractions allow us to control concrete fact. Over the past 40 years (or even 50 years, if his teenage recollections are reliable), Shaw's core abstractions have been symmetry and duality.

In common parlance, an object has *symmetry* if it is the same on one side as the other, typically, on both sides of a dividing line. In mathematics, an object has symmetry if it is the same on both sides of a transformation. More pointedly, certain transformations can be applied that leave an object unchanged, whereas other

Correspondence should be addressed to Claudia Carello, CESPA, Unit 1020, 406 Babbidge Road, University of Connecticut, Storrs, CT 06269–1020. E-mail: claudia.carello@uconn.edu

transformations change the object fundamentally. An object that has been transformed but retains its essential properties—that looks the same as it did before—is said to have symmetry. The relevance for psychology is that an emphasis on symmetry leads facts and theory, guides experimentation, and constrains explanation. Direct perception implies a symmetry. If it happens to be the right symmetry, then the path to the right theory of epistemic intentional agents will have been identified.

And what of duality? The common understanding of dual—having two similar parts or having a double nature—goes only so far. And we clearly do not want the more commonly used dualism that entails an irreducibility between the two aspects. *Duality*, in contrast, entails mutuality: Given two different systems, if you can obtain one by interchanging the elements or operations of the other, the systems have duality. The relevance for psychology is that an emphasis on duality reveals fundamental analogies between distinct and different things; it promises conceptual economy. *Organism–niche* implies a duality. Theorems proven about *organism* yield dual theorems that assert truths about *niche,* and vice versa; similarly, for perception theorems and action theorems. Duality is a nontransitive relation that expresses invariants and specificity and, therefore, no transitivity and no mediation.

Taken together, symmetry and duality provide a guiding context for an ecological approach to perception. Moreover, they are suited in style to Gibson's (1982) biases for that approach: "I prefer radical solutions to scientific problems whenever possible. General explanations are always preferable to piecemeal explanations ... and this is all that is meant by a radical theory" (p. 14). Shaw has long used the building blocks of symmetry and duality to ask radical questions inspiring radical—general, coherent—theory. In this first issue inspired by the symmetry and duality conference, several of these themes are illustrated historically, empirically, and critically.

Jenkins (this issue) begins this issue with a journey through the psychology of the late 20th century. He shows how the intellectual atmosphere at the University of Minnesota's Center for Research in Human Learning might encourage Shaw, a new PhD trained in neo-associationism, to discover his Shavian self. In providing a historical context for the other contributors, Jenkins allows us to see that Shaw was never a hit-and-run psychologist. The questions Shaw saw as important continued to fascinate him in refined guises throughout his career.

For example, is an *event* at the ecological scale so characterized by symmetries that the change and the nonchange can be separately and uniquely specified? Do events and and their perception lack a characteristic space–time scale so that slow events must be addressed in the same terms as fast events? These questions sit at the center of three contributions. Pittenger's (this issue) is a historical summary of what might be considered the defining research program of Shaw's career, the so-called face project. Pittenger evaluates the work against the standards of what he takes to constitute a complete ideal study of event perception. In a complementary reminiscence on the face project, Mark (this issue) focuses on the systematicity of the search for information in natural constraints. He then shows how this systematic approach has implicitly guided his own research into what he calls the ecology of sitting. Bingham (this issue) shows how the event perception framework provides a useful paradigm for space perception in his investigation of natural constraints on size. Time and again, these contributors illustrate Whitehead's (1925) assertion that abstractions—in this case, in the form of symmetry and duality—provide insight into, and thereby control over, the concrete.

The first four contributions are by "fellow travelers"—mentors, colleagues, and students of Shaw's. The final entry in this volume comes from the conference session dubbed "A View From the Outside." Wells (this issue) picks up on Shaw's critique of computational theory, particularly its failure to embody natural constraints that must be satisfied by real agents. This emphasis on algorists over algorithms led Shaw to question whether the internal states of computational machines might be substituted by dual perception and action histories without loss of formal functionality. Does the symmetry principle fixing direct perception have a dual, namely, a symmetry principle fixing direct intention? Wells argues that a rigorous account of the intentional agent is found in Turing.

Gibson (1982) once lamented that "Psychology ... is a second rate discipline. The main reason is that it does not *stand in awe* of its subject matter" (p. 1). As the articles here show, Shaw stands in awe of his subject matter, and that attitude has been delightfully contagious for generations.

REFERENCES

Gibson, J. J. (1967). James Gibson. In E. G. Boring & G. Lindzey (Eds.), *History of psychology in autobiography, Vol. 5* (pp. 125–144). New York: Appleton-Century-Crofts.

Gibson, J. J. (1972). A theory of direct visual perception. In J. Royce & W. Rozeboom (Eds.), *Psychology of knowing* (pp. 215–232). New York: Gordon & Breach.

Gibson, J. J. (1982). Autobiography. In E. S. Reed & R. Jones (Eds.), *Reasons for realism.* Englewood Cliffs, NJ: Lawrence Erlbaum Associates, Inc.

Whitehead, A. N. (1967). *Science and the modern world.* New York: Free Press. (Original work published 1925)

ECOLOGICAL PSYCHOLOGY, 17(3 & 4), 135–145
Copyright © 2005, Lawrence Erlbaum Associates, Inc.

ARTICLES

Robert E. Shaw:
The Minnesota Years: 1966–1975

James J. Jenkins

Department of Psychology
University of South Florida

After receiving his doctorate, Robert Shaw spent 10 years at the University of Minnesota, first as a postdoctoral fellow at the newly formed Center for Research in Human Learning, and then as a faculty member of the Department of Psychology. During that decade, Shaw and the Center profoundly influenced each other's development in many ways. This article briefly describes some events of that period.

Robert E. Shaw came to Minnesota on the recommendation of James Koplin, his adviser in psychology at Vanderbilt University. Koplin had mentored Shaw after his escape from an unfriendly philosophy department and saw that he was well trained (and published) in the "mediated association" approach to psychological theory, or, as it was sometimes called, "neo-associationism." It was a school of psychology descended from strict stimulus–response behaviorism via the theory of Clark Hull (Hull, 1943). It exploited the notions of implicit stimuli and responses operating in associative fashion to account for complex behaviors that obviously were not simple links between observable stimuli and responses. C. E. Osgood's massive book, *Method and Theory in Experimental Psychology*, summarized this view in 1953. Indeed, almost the entire last half of that book is an exercise in devising hypothetical accounts for complex behaviors via the mediational device. But the Minnesota to which Shaw came was not the same Minnesota from which Koplin had graduated a few years earlier; the Zeitgeist was rapidly changing.

It was Shaw's fortune (for good or ill) to become the first postdoctoral student in a new organization at Minnesota, The Center for Research in Human Learning.

Correspondence should be addressed to James J. Jenkins, 40 River Road, Apt. 14A, New York, NY 10044. E-mail: j3cube@aol.com

The newly formed center (now called the Center for Cognitive Sciences) was seeking a radical change away from association psychology. However, it was by no means a unified group of faculty and students. I, the brand new director of the center, was an ardent convert to Noam Chomsky's new movement in linguistics and was striving to discover what that meant for psychology. Herbert Pick from the Cornell background of MacLeod and the Gibsons brought a nontraditional perspective in perception, a topic that, prior to his arrival, had been virtually nonexistent at Minnesota. John Flavell had just arrived on the Minnesota scene as one of the leading American interpreters of Piaget. Milton Trapold, an Iowa-trained rigorously behavioristic learning theorist, was pushing the boundaries of neo-associationism and exploring the notion of "expectations" in animals. Paul Johnson, a Johns Hopkins PhD, was exploring word associations of physicists and their students. Russell Burris and Wells Hively were Skinnerian in orientation but concerned with learning in real settings of elementary and college classrooms. There were also a few old-fashioned functionalists who were simply concerned with all sorts of applied problems involving learning. Subjects in the various studies ranged from rats and goldfish, through babies and elementary schoolchildren, to mature adults. In short, the center being assembled was a tangle of views, goals, techniques, orientations, and opinions. All of us were struggling with our problems (and with each other) while waiting for some Alexander to cut the associative Gordian knot.

When Shaw arrived in the fall of 1966, I was scheduled to conduct a year-long seminar on the psychology of language. It met at 8:00 on Monday mornings in a large, cold room in the old psychology building. (The first arrival was charged with making an urn of black coffee for the others.) It was a remarkable seminar. Donald Foss and I were just back from a year at the Center for Advanced Study in the Behavioral Sciences in which we had been bludgeoned by the philosopher Jerry Fodor and the linguist Sol Saporta until we believed that we understood a really deep reading of Chomsky's (1957) *Syntactic Structures*. Consequently that little book was chosen to be the focus of the seminar.

Remarkably, the seminar was the only place on the Minnesota campus where a student could get any version of Chomsky. Because of that, the class had a strangely mixed enrollment of about 15 graduate students from anthropology, English, philosophy, foreign languages, and psychology. As it turned out, three of the psychologists were crucial to the functioning of the seminar: Don Foss, Terry Halwes, and Bob Shaw.

Why was a language seminar so important? David Palermo and I had worked out in detail how the neo-Hullian approach fitted exactly with the notion of language as a finite state grammar (see Jenkins & Palermo, 1964), and we conducted a lot of research to show that the mediated associative mechanisms could be counted on to do the task. (There were just a few problems to be worked out; see Jenkins, 1963). The "good news" was that the psychological theory meshed perfectly with an "item and arrangement" grammar (essentially a finite state grammar) that was the staple of American linguistics in the 1950s. The "bad news" was that Chomsky had just advanced a proof that a finite state grammar was not sufficient to account for natural language. If that were true, and by then we were convinced that it was, then neo-associationism was *in principle* not able to account for human language! Clearly, we were in a classic back-to-the-drawing-board situation.

All four of us psychologists had done successful research in mediated associations, hoping to build that case for understanding language, but now we saw disaster ahead. All of us were ready to undertake something new, but just what the something new was to be was not clear. We were convinced, however, that it had to be a radical departure from the associationistic past. Thus, the seminar was a mixture of sentence-by-sentence tutorial on Chomsky's (1957) *Syntactic Structures* to let everyone see what Foss and I thought we saw and background reading of Thomas Kuhn's (1962) *The Structure of Scientific Revolutions* to encourage everyone to break away from the past. The outcome was a set of stimulating rough-and-tumble discussions about how one might extend the generative approach to other classes of behaviors, how one might do "real" experiments on rule-governed behaviors, and how one might bring data into relation with hypothetical grammars and the like. It was a heady time, full of excitement and innovation.

Here is an example. One day in the seminar, Shaw asked if one could write a grammar of ellipses, that is, a grammar of acceptable sentence fragments. I replied, thoughtlessly, that one didn not need to. One just had a regular grammar and stopped or started arbitrarily. Shaw, Halwes, and Foss took that as a challenge, met that weekend, and devised an ellipsis grammar! Their grammar not only worked, it turned out to be the complement of a question grammar. (This is just as it should have been, when one gives the matter serious thought.) The fact that "the professor" could be so egregiously wrong was an inspiration to everyone and became one of the characteristic attitudes of the seminar and subsequently of the members of the center. Researchers who did not want to be questioned on fundamental issues began avoiding presentations at the center.

Over the course of the next year or so, largely under Shaw's guidance but with the ever-present contributions of Foss and Halwes, we developed the competence, automata, and performance (CAP) model as a framework to guide our research. We thought one should start with the development of competence models (e.g., Chomsky's grammar), experimentally study the relevant performance (people's language behavior), and, finally, develop a putative machine (an automaton) that could, in fact, bridge between the first and the second. (You can see the temporal order for the researcher should be C–P–A, but because we could not pronounce "CPA," we put the initials in a pronounceable order and called it "CAP.")

Perhaps I should explain the terms a little:

Competence: The basic idea was that one ought to develop "generative grammars for behavior," that is, rule-governed systems that adequately described the behaviors of interest, whether linguistic products, social behavior, cognition, morals, or what have you. The rules were to be idealized descriptions of the tacit knowledge of the behaver. Notice these are not *laws*, but *rules*. Presumably, in science you cannot violate a law or it would not be a law. You can, however, fail to follow rules for a multitude of reasons. One can compare our use of grammars with Wendell Garner's (1974) use of the notion of normative models.

Performance: This was the most psychological part of our thought. Here we argued that one must take into account the kinds of tasks the organisms were engaged in; the external supports and constraints that were involved; the background of knowledge and skills of the organism; the organism's memory, attention, and energy resources; the strategy employed; the materials available; and the like. That is to say that *performance* recognized the entire internal and external context of the organism. From our new point of view, we saw many other psychologists as building models of laboratory tasks, not models of minds, and, perhaps, failing to understand what they were doing.

Automata: This part of the model was uniquely due to Shaw with his interest in automata and relational algebras. Among other things, he impressed us with the notion of "mimicking automata." A complex machine may be programmed to act as a simpler machine and a simpler machine can (within limits) be programmed to deliver answers, say, from a table, that it is not programmed to compute. Examples of such machines are plentiful. Any complex machine or version of software that replaces its predecessor needs to be able to perform the programs of the earlier form, or we will spend all our time rewriting our applications every time we build a more powerful machine. Similarly, Shaw pointed out, experts might initially have to "compute" an answer to a particular type of problem. However, in the long run, they no longer need to compute; they just remember or recognize that what is before them is a case like those they have previously encountered. If one accepts this point of view, one recognizes that the human being is more like a universal machine that can become whatever kind of machine it needs to be for the particular problem in which it is engaged. Models of the mind, then, must recognize that minds can be different machines for different tasks, for different stages of development, and for different degrees of practice in the same task. Shaw gave three evening lectures to a packed classroom of faculty and graduate students espousing his ideas on these topics, and we were off and running.

The CAP model stimulated a plethora of discussions, experiments, and arguments. The students at the center were impressed enough and irreverent enough to erect a life-size statue of me, colored in bright orange Day-Glo paint, holding aloft a torch encircled with the letters C-A-P, and clutching a copy of *Syntactic Structures* (Chomsky, 1957) in my other hand!

Shaw did a little experiment (unpublished, of course) to demonstrate the modifiability of the human in a particular experimental situation. Each trial involved a small number of flashes of a red light followed by a white light, which was followed in turn by the same number of flashes of a green light. The number of flashes varied from trial to trial. The participant's task on each trial was to predict the next light. The participants quickly caught on and succeeded in predicting all the green lights in this task. Bob argued that, in principle, one didn't need to be as complex as a counting machine; one could simply be a "push-down store." (A push-down store is like a plate server in a cafeteria. You put a stack of plates in and the customers take them out until they are all gone. The server doesn't need to know how many plates it is holding. It just stops when the last plate is out.) In this experiment, it can be that simple. So many red lights in and so many taps for green lights out. But the participant does not need to know how many, just that it is the same. Bob ran his participants for many trials and then suddenly, after a string of red lights, he would ask, "How many red lights were there?" Sure enough, the participants had to run off a series of taps to count them and say how many there were. They had begun acting like a simpler machine. Our conjecture was that with sufficient experience experimental participants would become the simplest machine they could be to handle a given experimental problem. This led us to the ungenerous conclusion that, if one's model of the mind led one to run stupid experiments, participants would comply and act like stupid machines. In this way an experiment designed with a simple theory of mind could "create" the appropriate behavior in the participant to verify the theory. So much for modeling the mind with simple experiments!

About this time, Thomas Hyde and I stumbled into an experiment that showed that the tasks that participants were performing when they encountered a list of words determined whether they remembered the words later (Hyde & Jenkins, 1969). It did not matter whether they were given instructions to learn or not. The type of task determined the recall, not the participant's intention. With some instructions, it was as if the participants had not even heard the list; with other instructions the learning was superior to what the participants could do on their own, even when they knew they were going to be tested later. What the participant was doing with the material was the controlling factor. Walter Reitman, who came to teach a summer course for us, reinforced our belief that psychologists who were building models of "memory" were actually building models of particular tasks, not models of minds.

As must be readily apparent, we concluded that we could not contemplate creating a "grand theory." As we worked more and more on a variety of problems, we found that they had to be dealt with on their own terms. Eventually, we came to believe that we were developing a kind of *contextual functionalism*. We got the label "contextualism" from Stephen Pepper (1942) and the "functionalism" from the long tradition of American psychology, from the prevailing attitude of Minnesota's applied psychology, and from the kinds of real problems that we sought to investigate. I spoke briefly on this topic (Jenkins, 1974), but it is my hope that at some point Shaw will give this position the careful treatment that it deserves. We encouraged the students at the center to find ecologically valid problems that were interesting, important, and tractable, although we could not tell them how to ensure the last! The stress on "ecological validity" foreshadowed the move on Bob's part toward a Gibsonian perspective that was to dominate his later work.

Looking back at Shaw's 10 years at Minnesota I am amazed by the originality, the breadth, and the depth of his activities. I find it hard to believe that he could compress so much activity into 10 years. Here are some examples.

In 1967, Shaw became a consultant to Hildred Schuell's aphasia clinic at the Minneapolis Veterans Hospital. There he began to develop a psycholinguistic view of aphasia (Schuell, Shaw, & Brewer, 1969; Sefer & Shaw, 1972) and became a co-author of the book that summarized Schuell's contributions to research and treatment of aphasia (Jenkins, Jimenez-Pabon, Shaw, & Sefer, 1975). He and I further collaborated on a chapter arguing for the nonarbitrariness of the relation between speech and language (Jenkins & Shaw, 1975).

At a meeting in 1967, I became fascinated with Posner's report of his experiment on the genesis of abstract ideas (Posner & Keele, 1968). The experiment presented distortions of three different random patterns of dots. After learning labels for sets of these distorted patterns, the participants transferred the labels to new distortions of the patterns and to the original patterns themselves (the "prototypes" they had never seen).

We set up a successful replication at Minnesota (Strange, Keeney, Kessel, & Jenkins, 1970), but as we ran ourselves and others in the experiment, we were puzzled. Statistically, it was clear that we apprehended at least something of what had generated the sets of abstract patterns that constituted the stimuli in the experiment. However, we had no "feeling of knowing" the prototypes and no clear idea of what it was we were supposed to know. John Bransford and Jeffrey Franks, students at the center who had this experience as participants in the experiment, were in one of Shaw's seminars in which they considered the matter. Shaw, of course, urged them to consider it at a more abstract level. When they did, they came to believe that the trouble with the Posner–Keele experiment was in the kinds of "transformations" employed. The instances of the random dot patterns that the participants saw were changed from the prototype by greater or lesser random perturbations of the individual dots, the smallest elements of the prototype. The instances did not involve geometric transformations of structural components of the prototypes. In short, there could be only statistical approximations; there were no systematic transformations to apprehend.

Franks and Bransford then devised tasks involving global transformations of configurations of geometric shapes and got outstanding results. Participants in their experiments not only recognized the prototype that they had never seen but also could draw it spontaneously (Franks & Bransford, 1971)! Then Bransford and Franks (1971) extended their work by analogy to sentences and startled psychologists and psycholinguists everywhere with the demonstration that the business of the head was not to record pieces, or elements, or atoms, or even particular stimuli, but to synthesize experience into coherent wholes.

Shaw and Wilson (1976) returned to an old experiment by Esper (1925) on miniature linguistic systems to make a far-reaching claim. Foss (1968) had shown that the Esper stimuli could be described by a little grammar and that what the participants learned was compatible with the idea that they had learned the grammar rather than a series of stimulus–response connections. Shaw, in his typical fashion, elevated this to an even more general level exploiting suggestions by the mathematician Poincaré, the physicist Helmholtz, and the philosopher Cassirer that mathematical group structure was the important determiner of generalization. If the learner saw instances of some pattern in which the instances constituted "group generators," he or she generalized to the complete set, whereas if the learner saw an equal number of instances but they were not group generators, there was no generalization to the remaining members of the set. Shaw's work here stimulated several sets of studies on the perception and recognition of pictorial events and the recognition of geometric patterns (see Jenkins & Tuten, 1998; Jenkins, Wald, & Pittenger, 1978).

The center frequently sponsored summer programs that would stretch our minds and attitudes. One summer session had a great impact on many of us and on Shaw in particular. The center hosted both James J. and Eleanor J. Gibson from Cornell and Alvin M. Liberman from Haskins Laboratories. It was a summer rich in perception of all varieties. J. J. Gibson was in the midst of his last book and his seminar went through the drafts chapter by chapter. The students had some impact on the final form of the book, and Gibson had a great impact on Shaw as well as others. Shaw and Gibson spent hours outside of class in discussion and argument. For Bob, trained in philosophy as well as psychology, it was a rare opportunity to explore Gibson's variety of direct realism and what it meant for a psychology of perception and action. The interaction later led to the invitation for Shaw to spend a year at Cornell where he taught Gibson's course in perception, tutored by Jimmy himself. When Shaw returned to Minnesota, he began teaching a perception course in the psychology department, in which such a course had been on the books for years but had not been taught in anyone's memory.

When Peter Pufall arrived at the center as a postdoctoral student, he and Shaw undertook a series of studies of Piagetian tasks on children's apprehension of space and number. These studies challenged the ideas that many of us had about the development of these concepts. Indeed, it appeared that many abstractions were available to the developing child when tested singly, but "honoring" more than one or two aspects at a time was not yet possible (see the studies by Pufall & Shaw, 1972, 1973; Pufall, Shaw, & Syrdal-Lasky, 1973). Pufall later wrote (personal communication, December, 2004)

> The work that we did shifted in two short years from an effort to merge Chomsky and Piaget by writing different grammars to capture changes in children's under-

standing ... to merging Piaget and Gibson on the relation of our perception and conception of reality. ... We hoped that our experiments on space and number would yield some insights into the way perceptual information structured thought and its development rather than accepting the prevailing idea that thought filled in impoverished perception.

As a result of pondering the question of the perception of change, John Pittenger and Shaw began their famous series of studies exploring Shaw's idea that the change of head shape with age could be mapped with a global transformation. They demonstrated that the transformation was seen by humans as the slow change in the age of the target, whether the target was human or lower animal, or even inanimate, like a Volkswagen car (see Pittenger & Shaw, 1974, 1975a, 1975b; Shaw & Pittenger, 1977)!

Toward the end of his stay at Minnesota, Shaw began writing and publishing his thoughts on symmetry and on how cognition should be treated within the nexus of automata theory. Stimulated by von Neumann's conjectures concerning complexity, he examined the notion of complexity and what it might have to do with our studies of cognitive processes. He and Michael McIntyre outlined the problem of the algorist, and they, along with William Mace, started examining the notion of symmetry and its role in cognition and perception. These articles, of course, were only the beginning of what was to be an extensive contribution to this literature (see Shaw & McIntyre, 1974; Shaw, McIntyre, & Mace, 1974).

It is apparent that, in addition to his particular efforts in research and theory, Shaw furnished stimulating leadership for others and led in the development of an orienting philosophy of the center. Surprisingly, beyond that, Shaw consulted with an amazing variety of institutions and projects—the Minneapolis Institute of Art, Russ Burris's foreign language teaching project, the Instruction Design Group, Minnesota Systems Research, the Aphasia Clinic, and a Title III grant in an elementary school. He also found time to win a career development award from The National Institute of Child Health and Human Development and to write grants for special summer programs for the center as well as the renewal of the general center grant and the center training grant.

Shaw's impact on the University of Minnesota is readily apparent from the following facts: After his postdoctoral fellowship, he was invited to stay on at Minnesota as an assistant professor. (The retention of a postdoctoral fellow as a faculty member was an event unprecedented in the history of the psychology department and, to the best of my knowledge, it is still a unique occurrence.) In 3 more years he was made an associate professor and in another 4 years he was a full professor. He was coauthor of one book, coeditor of another, had published eight book chapters, nine journal articles, had been involved in 14 conferences, and had given 20 invited addresses at other institutions. While making this rapid ascent, he had somehow managed to spend a year at the Center for Advanced Study in the Behavioral Sciences and a year as a visiting professor at Cornell University. He had also spent a summer at the University of California at Los Angeles at the Linguistic Institute and a brief residency at the Institute for Theoretical Psychology in Canada! He had launched a number of graduate students on the path to their degrees and had stimulated the entire group of faculty in four departments at the center. It was, indeed, a meteoric beginning of his outstanding career.

A FINAL WORD

No account of Shaw's Minnesota years would be complete without some mention of the more personal side of the man. Once he began talking about psychology, he became a classic absent-minded professor. He frequently drove me home from the university, but sometimes that event was full of surprises. On one awful night as we walked through the harsh winter winds from the center to the parking lots, Shaw was, of course, talking all the time. As we passed the last parking lot, I pointed out that fact to him. "Oh my gosh!" he said, "I've forgotten where I parked the car!" On another occasion, it turned out even worse. There was no car at all! He had parked on the other campus and taken the bus. It was always interesting, but somewhat dangerous, to rely on him for transportation.

True to his nature, Bob could never resist rising to the most abstract level at which he could consider a problem. Consequently, in his classes, regardless of the particular topic on which he was lecturing, he was likely to ascend to an abstract plane and consider the most general class of problems of the sort he was contemplating, leaving the students struggling valiantly in their attempt to keep up with him. A common question to ask when one saw his students coming out of class was, "Did Shaw 'vroom ' today?" And the most common answer was, "Yeah, he really 'vroomed'!"

That may be the ultimate description of Bob Shaw's 10 years at Minnesota. He really VROOMED!

ACKNOWLEDGMENT

In the preparation of this article I was assisted by Donald Foss, Terry Halwes, Herbert Pick, John Pittenger, Peter Pufall, and Winifred Strange. They tried to remind me of that "golden decade" and to keep me from error. Any omissions or errors remaining are entirely my fault.

REFERENCES

Bransford, J. D., & Franks, J. J. (1971). The abstraction of linguistic ideas. *Cognitive Psychology, 2*, 331–350.

Chomsky, N. (1957). *Syntactic structures*. The Hague, Netherlands: Mouton.

Esper, E. A. (1925). A technique for experimental investigation of associative interference in artificial linguistic materials. *Language Monographs, 1*.

Foss, D. J. (1968). An analysis of learning in a miniature linguistic system. *Journal of Experimental Psychology, 76*, 450–459.

Franks, J. J., & Bransford, J. D. (1971). Abstraction of visual patterns. *Journal of Experimental Psychology, 90*, 65–74.

Garner, W. R. (1974). *The processing of information and structure*. Hillsdale, NJ: Lawrence Erlbaum Associates, Inc.

Gibson, J. J. (1979). *The ecological approach to visual perception*. Boston: Houghton-Mifflin.

Hull, C. L. (1943). *Principles of behavior.* New York: Appleton-Century-Crofts.

Hyde, T. S., & Jenkins, J. J. (1969). Differential effects of incidental tasks on the organization of recall of a list of highly associated words. *Journal of Experimental Psychology, 82*, 472–481.

Jenkins, J. J. (1963). Mediated associations: Paradigms and situations. In C. N. Cofer & B. S. Musgrave (Eds.), *Verbal behavior and learning* (pp. 210–245). New York: McGraw-Hill.

Jenkins, J. J. (1974). Remember that old theory of memory? Well, forget it! *American Psychologist, 29*, 785–795.

Jenkins, J. J., Jimenez-Pabon, E., Shaw, R. E., & Sefer, J. (1975). *Schuell's aphasia in adults*. New York: Harper & Row.

Jenkins, J. J., & Palermo, D. S. (1964). Mediation processes and the acquisition of linguistic structure. In U. Bellugi & R. W. Brown (Eds.), *The acquisition of language. Monographs of the Society for Research in Child Development, 29*(1, Serial No. 92).

Jenkins, J. J., & Shaw, R. E. (1975). On the interrelatedness of speech and language. In J. Cavanaugh & J. Cutting (Eds.), *The role of speech in language*. Cambridge, MA: MIT Press.

Jenkins, J. J., & Tuten, J. T. (1998). On possible parallels between perceiving and remembering events. In R. R. Hoffman, M. F. Sherrick, & J. S. Warm (Eds.), *Viewing psychology as a whole: The integrative science of William N. Dember* (pp. 291–314). Washington, DC: American Psychological Association.

Jenkins, J. J., Wald, J., & Pittenger, J. B. (1978). Apprehending pictorial events: An instance of psychological cohesion. In C. W. Savage (Ed.), *Cognition and perception: Issues in the philosophy of psychology. Minnesota studies in the philosophy of science, Vol. 9* (pp. 129–163). Minneapolis: University of Minnesota Press.

Kuhn, T. S. (1962). *The structure of scientific revolutions*. Chicago: University of Chicago Press.

Mace, W. M., & Shaw, R. E. (1974). Simple kinetic information for transparent depth. *Perception & Psychophysics, 15*, 201–209.

Osgood, C. E. (1953). *Method and theory in experimental psychology*. New York: Oxford University Press

Pepper, S. C. (1942). *World hypotheses*. Berkeley: University of California Press.

Pittenger, J. B., & Shaw, R. E. (1974). Perceiving age in facial profiles. In J. Scandura, J. Durnin, & W. Wulfeck (Eds.), *1974 proceedings: Fifth Annual Interdisciplinary Conference on Structural Learning*. Narberth, PA: MERGE Research Institute.

Pittenger, J. B., & Shaw, R. E. (1975a). Aging faces as viscal-elastic events: Implications for a theory of non-rigid shape perception. *Journal of Experimental Psychology: Human Performance and Perception, 1*, 374–382.

Pittenger, J. B., & Shaw, R. E. (1975b). Perception of relative and absolute age in facial photographs. *Perception & Psychophysics, 18*, 137–143.

Posner, M. I., & Keele, S. W. (1968). On the genesis of abstract ideas. *Journal of Experimental Psychology, 77*, 353–363.

Pufall, P., & Shaw, R. E. (1972). Some precocious thoughts on number: The long and the short of it. *Developmental Psychology, 7*, 62–69.

Pufall, P., & Shaw, R. E. (1973). An analysis of the development of children's spatial reference system. *Journal of Cognitive Psychology, 5*, 151–175.

Pufall, P., Shaw, R. E., & Syrdal-Lasky, A. (1973). Development of number conservation: An examination of some predictions from Piaget's stage analysis and equilibration. *Journal of Experimental Child Development, 44,* 21–27.

Schuell, H., Shaw, R. E., & Brewer, W. (1969). Psycholinguistic study of the aphasic deficit. *Journal of Speech and Hearing Research, 12,* 794–806.

Sefer, J., & Shaw, R. E. (1972). Psycholinguistics and aphasia. *British Journal of Disorders in Communication, 3,* 87–89.

Shaw, R. E. (1969). Cognition, simulation and the problem of complexity. *Journal of Structural Learning, 2,* 31–44.

Shaw, R. E. (1973). Simulation and the problem of complexity. In J. Scandura (Ed.), *Structural learning.* New York: Gordon & Breach.

Shaw, R. E., & Bransford, J. (Eds.). (1977a). *Perceiving, acting, and knowing: Toward an ecological psychology.* Hillsdale, NJ: Lawrence Erlbaum Associates, Inc.

Shaw, R. E., & Bransford, J. (1977b). Psychological approaches to the problem of knowledge. In R. E. Shaw & J. Bransford (Eds.), *Perceiving, acting, and knowing: Toward an ecological psychology* (pp. 1–39). Hillsdale, NJ: Lawrence Erlbaum Associates, Inc.

Shaw, R. E., & McIntyre, M. (1974). Algoristic foundations for cognitive psychology. In W. Weimer & D. Palermo (Eds.), *Cognition and symbolic processes* (pp. 306–362). Hillsdale, NJ: Lawrence Erlbaum Associates, Inc.

Shaw, R. E., McIntyre, M., & Mace, W. M. (1974). The role of symmetry in event perception. In H. Pick & R. MacLeod (Eds.), *Studies in perception: Essays in honor of J. J. Gibson* (pp. 276–310). Ithaca, NY: Cornell University Press.

Shaw, R. E., & Pittenger, J. B. (1977). Perceiving the face of change in changing faces: Implications for a theory of object perception. In R. E. Shaw & J. Bransford (Eds.), *Perceiving, acting, and knowing: Toward an ecological psychology* (pp. 103–132). Hillsdale, NJ: Lawrence Erlbaum Associates, Inc.

Shaw, R. E., & Wilson, B. (1976). Abstract conceptual knowledge: How we know what we know. In D. Klahr (Ed.), *Cognition and instruction: 10th Annual Carnegie-Mellon Symposium on Information Processing* (pp. 197–221). Hillsdale, NJ: Lawrence Erlbaum Associates, Inc.

Strange, W., Keeney, T., Kessel, F. S., & Jenkins, J. J. (1970). Abstraction over time of prototypes from distortions of random dot patterns: A replication. *Journal of Experimental Psychology, 83,* 508–510.

ECOLOGICAL PSYCHOLOGY, 17(3 & 4), 147–159
Copyright © 2005, Lawrence Erlbaum Associates, Inc.

The Early Years of Robert Shaw's Craniofacial Growth Project

John B. Pittenger

Department of Psychology
University of Arkansas at Little Rock

The early years of Robert Shaw's long series of studies of the perception of growth are summarized. This body of work, when compared to an ideal set of ecological studies of event perception, misses some components. However, it is among the most successful bodies of ecological research, one involving an unusually wide variety of disciplines in addition to psychology. The scope and success of the project reflect the breadth and depth of Shaw's intellectual interests.

Robert Shaw's research into craniofacial growth and the perception of age was an exceptionally successful project, both as an example of research guided by the ecological approach to perception and as a set of studies into the perception of an event. It consisted of an unusually broad set of experiments—ones that are necessary to a full understanding of the perception of an event, but that are rarely conducted. In this article I describe the work done in the early years of the project, trying to explain how the project developed over time. The project is compared to what I take to be an ideal set of studies into the perception of an event. I conclude that Shaw's project was uniquely complete compared to other event research, yet did not entirely meet the requirements of an ideal event perception project. A central theme in this article will be that Shaw's wide variety of intellectual interests was central to the project's evolution.

THE IDEAL EVENT PERCEPTION PROJECT

The success of the face project can best be evaluated by comparing its results to those of an ideal event perception project guided by the ecological approach. An

Correspondence should be addressed to John B. Pittenger, Department of Psychology, University of Arkansas at Little Rock, 2801 S. University Ave., Little Rock, AR 72204. E-mail: jbpittenger@ualr.edu

ideal project would consist of three phases: documentation of perception of the event in everyday life, discovery of the information available to perceivers, and documentation that the information is picked up by perceivers and is used by them in perceiving the event.

The first component would, at the very least, demonstrate that the event is perceived. In addition, there could be assessments of the accuracy with which it is perceived, the degree of individual differences in perception, and so on. In other words, the researcher would document the phenomenon that the rest of the project will attempt to explain. This documentation should include the perception of the objects engaged in the event. In many events the objects, although transformed by the event, retain their perceived identities. For example, a chair after being painted is still the same chair. In some events identity is not preserved: If the chair were to be burnt, then the resulting pile of ashes is not the chair. Thus the documentation phase of an ideal project could include assessment of the preservation of perceived identities of participating objects once they are transformed by the event.

Second, the researcher needs to discover what information supporting the perception of the event is available in sensory arrays. Because events involve change, the information for event perception must lie in patterns of change. Shaw has called these patterns *transformational invariants.* This term involves two ideas. The use of *transformation* obviously refers to the changes wrought by the event. The use of *invariant* is theoretically loaded in that it claims that the same pattern of change occurs in every instance of the event. That is, the same event is perceived because the same event is actually occurring. In addition, Shaw used the term *structural invariant.* The idea here was that, as objects are changed by an event, some aspects of those objects do not change. The structures that do not change are precisely those believed by ecological psychologists to constitute the information for the perception of an object's identity as an event transpires.

Third, the researcher needs to demonstrate that the available information is actually picked up by perceivers and that pickup leads to perceptual experiences very similar to those in everyday life. Displays are created in which the transformational invariant is applied to the appropriate object or objects, then the participants are asked, directly or indirectly, what they perceive. Finally, the researcher needs to access the preservation of the identities of the objects in these displays. That is, he or she needs to find out whether or not the structural invariants carry the information for identity available in the event as it occurs in nature.

My emphasis on the first component comes from a principle that James J. Jenkins taught his students at the Center for Research in Human Learning: A good way to get started in research is to find a phenomenon to explain. I have interpreted this to mean that you should not simply create a study whose results would be consistent with the theory you held. Rather, you ought to try to explain something that happens in the real world. Perception researchers often neglect this step, leaving themselves in the somewhat odd position of developing theories without knowing much about the phenomena that those theories purport to explain. I have sometimes forgotten this advice, creating studies that allowed me to verify ecological ideas rather than to see how well I could account for a phenomenon using ecological principles.

Some historical context may help demonstrate the importance of Shaw's creation of structural invariants as a concept in ecological theory. It is important to remember that in the 1970s the study of event perception presented a new challenge to researchers: the need for the researcher to develop a precise description of the external environment being perceived. In motion perception studies there is no puzzle as to the changes occurring in the environment: A rotation is just a rotation. Thus, the specification of visual information involved in the projection of patterns of light to the optic array is so simple that it need not be made explicit. However, in event perception, the analysis of information includes specification of patterns in the environment itself. For example, to understand perception of the event walking, the researcher will need to say just what pattern of limb motions (i.e., what transformational invariant) constitutes walking, as opposed to, say, running. This new problem was widely understood at the time. It was not, however, generally recognized that these changes in the environment produced a second problem—preservation of perceived identity over those changes. Shaw's postulation of the existence of structural invariants claims that identity is perceived to persist because identity actually does persist: There are visible aspects of the object that do not change. This problem does not arise in traditional studies of motion perception because the rigid translations and rotations change only an object's location in space. Preservation of identity hardly seems to need explanation in this case. Shaw's notion of structural invariants provides Gibson's perceptual realism with a way to encompass a new class of phenomena. This concept merits more attention than it has received.

CONTEXT

The face project developed in the early 1970s at the University of Minnesota's Center for Research in Human Leaning, where Shaw and I were working. The intellectual climate at the center was crucial to the development of the face project.

Because Jim Jenkins (this issue) has provided an excellent survey of the intellectual developments at the Center for Research in Human Learning, I will mention only a few items central to the face project. First, there was the concern with what might be characterized as "instances and wholes." For example, many of us were interested in transformational psycholinguistics and the problem of how children could develop grammar on the basis of individual sentences. In addition, there was the question of how a category, say mammal, might arise from seeing a number of individual cats, dogs, etc. Memory was also being studied at the center. Up to that time memory research had focused on recall and recognition of individual items that had been presented previously; words, nonsense syllables, pictures, and so on. People at the Center realized that memory often contained meaningful wholes extracted from individual items in addition to the items themselves.

The groundbreaking studies by John Bransford and Jeff Franks (1971) developed out of these ideas. They showed that people who heard statements such as "The jelly was on the table," "The ants ate the jelly," and "The jelly was sweet" would later believe that they had heard "The ants ate the sweet jelly on the table." These "false recognitions" were viewed not as errors but as one of the major tasks that cognitive processes had to accomplish. Each sentence used by Bransford and Franks specified a particular event. Thus, as their participants heard the sentences, each of which described a component of an event, they apprehended and remembered the whole event. In the memory phase of the study they included that whole in their memories of what they heard.

Jim Jenkins and some of his students (Jenkins, Wald, & Pittenger, 1978) applied a variation of the Bransford–Franks paradigm to visual memory. In the learning phases of the studies participants were shown still photographs taken as an event transpired. For example, pictures taken as the photographer walked about a college campus. In the recognition phase they were presented with pictures they had previously seen, additional photographs taken during the walk, and other pictures of the campus not showing the path taken during the walk. Participants thought they had previously seen both new and old walk pictures but not the nonwalk ones. That is, they extracted the walk event from the pictures shown in the learning phase and then had difficulty remembering precisely what individual "pieces" of the event they had actually seen.

At this same time people at the center were becoming aware of James Gibson's (1979/1986) and Gunnar Johansson's (1973) work on the perception of events. These ideas, in conjunction with work like that of Bransford and Franks, led some of us, especially Bob Shaw, to suppose that events were of primary importance to both cognition and perception: Because everyday life is composed of events, it is reasonable to expect that the human mind would have developed sophisticated ways to apprehend them. We were not, of course, the only group of psychologists then thinking about events. However, most others saw perception and cognition as entirely separate systems, with perception being concerned with events that are happening now and cognition with past events.

Shaw and I distinguished between fast and slow events. *Fast events* are those in which the changes constituting the event occur fast enough that *both* the event and motion are perceived. In *slow events* the rate of change is slow enough that, although the event can be perceived, motion is not. For example, the movement of the second hand on a clock is a fast event whereas the movement of the hour hand is a slow one. We thought that it was not justified to simply assume that these two types of events were psychologically different, with only fast events being able to be perceived. In other words, we thought that event perception was not simply a subtype of motion perception.

The idea that slow events could be perceived was not universally accepted, even by some of our intellectual allies. Gunnar Johansson certainly thought that the face studies were matters of cognition rather than perception. I was surprised that, at least in my discussions with him, Jimmy Gibson did not seem fully convinced that slow events could be perceived.

Outside of the center there was little interest in events and their perception. In the early 1970s experimental psychology journals were publishing many studies of perceived motion per se, but little on perception of events, that is, situations in which some specific object is engaged in some specific activity. The event studies being discussed at the center at that time were few: the classic work of Michotte (1963) on causality, the work of Heider and Simmel (1944), Gunnar Johannson's (1973) studies of "point light" people, and some work out of Jimmy Gibson's laboratory (e.g., Gibson, Kaplan, Reynolds, & Wheeler, 1969). In addition, theories of event perception were just beginning to be developed.

WHAT WE DID

In the early 1970s Bob Shaw was deeply engaged in the attempt to develop a systematic mathematical basis for the transformations and the invariants under transformation. As part of this work he had been considering the growth of the human head. He wished to discover the transformations of the head and face that could account for our ability to make accurate estimates of other people's ages. I believe that several of Shaw's long-term interests led to the selection of facial growth as an event to study. First, his interests in mathematics that led him to read D'Arcy Thompson's (1917/1942) book *On Growth and Form*. Thompson used spatial coordinate transformations as a way to characterize the nonrigid patterns of growth. These transformations seemed to provide a mathematical approach to the characterization of some of the transformational invariants needed by ecologists. Shaw also had a serious interest in art and had long thought about the problem of representing a three-dimensional, dynamic world in two-dimensional, static media. In particular, he was aware of artists' needs to convey a person's age in drawings and paintings: What aspects of facial shape did artists manipulate so as to make the person appear to be of a particular age?

After a good deal of thought and study of mathematics and art books Shaw discovered two transformations that, together, seemed to capture the pattern of craniofacial growth. The first, cardioidal strain, stretched the face downward and outward, whereas the second, affine shear, acted so as to make the jaw protrude and the forehead slant backwards. These transformations were applied to an outline profile drawing of a human head and presented to participants in an age-estimation task. The resulting drawings appeared to produce changes in the apparent age of the person represented. This work is reported in Shaw, McIntyre, and Mace (1974).

At about this time I had returned to Minnesota after a yearlong postdoctoral fellowship with J. J. Gibson. The face work fascinated me: It opened a new class of events to study, looked to be a good place to apply Gibson's (1979/1986) ecological approach, had interesting mathematical aspects, and provided a variety of challenges for the design of experiments. I signed on, unknowingly commencing a wonderful intellectual adventure.

Shaw and I first redid the earlier study with new tasks for the participants and with new displays. The facial profiles in the original study had a somewhat unnatural appearance. Using the same transformations we varied the initial angular orientation of the face until the transformed faces looked more natural.

In one study (Experiment 1 in Pittenger & Shaw, 1975a) participants viewed a set of faces produced by these transformations and made magnitude estimates of the ages they portrayed (Figure 1). The results confirmed our predictions: As the profiles were transformed in the direction we believed to capture growth, they were estimated to be progressively older. This study is part of what I earlier called the

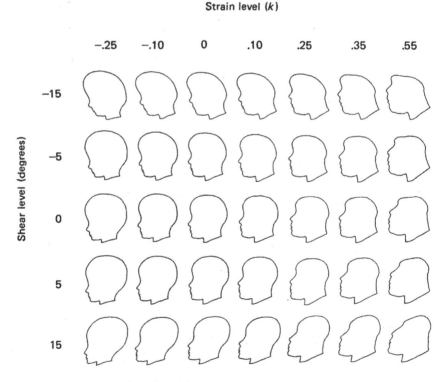

FIGURE 1   An array of transformed faces (reprinted from Pittenger & Shaw, 1975a, with permission).

second component of an ideal project: demonstration that the transformational invariant actually influences perception. Note that we did not ask those participants, "What seems to be happening?" Thus, these results showed that participants could interpret the results of these two transformations as aging, but did not address the question of how realistic those changes looked.

Shaw, I, and our participants noticed that strain clearly "went too far" in this set of profiles. Large negative values of strain produced foreheads that seemed far too large and faces that seemed too small. The reverse was true for large positive strains. We initially were concerned that these facts cast doubt on the validity of our transformations. Then Shaw realized that these could be viewed as "supernormal" stimuli, ones that according to ethologists (Lorenz, 1943) produced exaggerated responses. This explanation was not fully satisfactory because the extreme faces did not really look to be abnormally old or young—rather they seemed to look like something different, as if a continuous change in the display was producing a nearly categorical change in perception. Later, we (well, I bet it was really Shaw) realized that we inadvertently created an instance of neoteny. The term *neoteny* refers to the idea that adults of a more highly evolved species can have the characteristics of younger members of a less evolved species. See Gould (1987) for an introduction of this idea. Among our profiles, those with high positive degrees of strain look more like primitive hominids than very old humans, and those with high negative strain look like the hyperintelligent creatures from outer space as portrayed in some science fiction movies.

Finally, the data clearly showed that strain had a much greater impact on perceived age than did shear. However, we continued to employ shear in some later studies.

We only concluded one study Pittenger & Shaw, 1975a) that addressed the issue of structural invariance. We knew that, within limits, people continue to be identifiable as they grow. Therefore, our proposed transformational invariant of growth needed to preserve perceived identity. We considered applying strain, the more powerful transformation, to drawings of the faces of different individuals and asking whether or not participants could identify the different versions of each individual's face. In thought experiments conducted on ourselves this test seemed too easy to be convincing. Individual differences in eyes, mouths, and so on, are so great that we expected that participants would make few mistakes. To make the test more challenging, we traced a portion of the skulls shown in profile X-rays of the heads of six children. Specifically, we traced braincases—the line starting at the concave area at the top of the nose, going along the skull's midline to the point where the spine enters the skull. Five levels of strain were applied to each tracing. Slides were produced, each showing one braincase at the top and two on the bottom. One of the bottom braincases was a transformed version of the individual represented in the top drawing, whereas the other was that of a second individual. Participants were asked to pick the drawing on the bottom that showed the same individual as the one at the top. Because the majority of the choices were correct, we concluded that strain did preserve individual identity. We did not, however, try to discover precisely which aspects of the braincases' shapes carried the information for individual identity.

The innovative nature of Shaw's ideas is indicated by the fact that it was perfectly reasonable to present undergraduates with a perceptual task involving drawings of braincases traced from X-rays. Many nonecological people at the center saw the face project as a bit odd and, in some sense, not really psychology. The mathematics of growth was certainly the province of biologists, not psychologists. Moreover, they thought that there was no point in studying the perception of braincases because they are seen only by specialists such as radiologists and anthropologists.

At about this time we conducted our only study aimed at documenting the existence of the phenomenon we were studying: age perception (Pittenger & Shaw, 1975b). During a Center seminar at which Shaw and I were presenting our work, an enthusiastically nonecological faculty member asked us if we had a basis for thinking that people really did perceive each other's ages. My own initial reaction was that the question was silly: Everyone knows that we can perceive age. However, we did realize that some documentation of the accuracy with which age was perceived was needed. In addition, we were fully aware that variables other than shape change as one ages; skin coarsens, males develop beards, and so on. Shaw found a private school whose yearbooks contained photographs of individual students at each grade from 7th to 12th. We copied these and made sets of photos, each containing one face from each grade. Both longitudinal and cross-sectional sets were produced. Some sets showed the entire head and shoulders, others had the hair, neck, and shoulders but not the jawline masked out, whereas in the third set the jawline was also masked. Participants both made estimates of absolute age and ranked the faces by age. As expected, rankings and age estimates were quite accurate for the unmasked faces. Increasing masking reduced accuracy, suggesting that factors other than the structural changes of growth influence perceived age.

At this point we became interested in the generality of strain and shear. If they really were transformational invariants for growth, then transforming any of the members of the appropriate class of objects by them should produce the appearance of growth. We were convinced that this class contained all normally growing human faces, but wondered if it were broader. (Shaw was now at the University of Connecticut and Len Mark, Jim Todd, Tom Alley, and others were joining the project. The word we will now include them.)

We had so far transformed only a single human profile and an outline one at that. In part, this was because it seemed obvious to us that the same changes in perceived age would occur for any human profile we might use. In addition, we were constrained by the primitive computers then available: We gave the programmer the specifications of the face and transformations, and days later received drawings produced by a pen-and-ink plotter. These were then sent off to be photographed onto 2 in. × 2 in. slides. It was very confining compared to our current ability to produce displays rapidly on our own desktop computers.

Ethologists had made the point that in all species adults must be able to recognize the young of their species so that they can act appropriately toward them (Lorenz, 1943). Recalling that many baby animals appeared cute to humans, we speculated that animal faces, especially faces of mammals, might grow in a fashion similar to that of humans. This led us to wonder if applying strain and shear to animal faces would produce apparent growth. Detailed, realistic drawings of animal faces would be impractical to employ—because of computer limitations. Therefore, we used cartoon-style profile drawings of a dog, a monkey, and a bird. The use of cartoon drawings was justified by the fact that cartoonists are able to make animals appear as babies, adolescents, and adults. Among Bob Shaw's artistic interests was the question of how cartoonists and caricaturists are able to give objects perceptually convincing properties such as age when those objects are drawn in a style that is not entirely realistic. His idea was that these artists have discovered, often tacitly, the transformational and structural invariants of real events and objects and incorporate them into their drawings. In the case of growth and aging Shaw was convinced that cartoonists manipulated the shapes of heads and faces to achieve these effects. Thus, even if animal growth were not exactly like that of humans, participants might see growth when cartoon profiles were transformed. Using sets of drawings and tasks like those used in the study with the human profiles, our participants gave age estimates that were again strongly influenced by strain and shear.

As with the human profiles, shear was not nearly as effective as strain. Later math and physics work showed that shear was not needed to capture actual physical growth. It seems impressive that our participants' perceptual skills were so subtle: They realized the weakness of shear before Shaw and I did.

Continuing our investigation of the class of objects in which strain produces apparent growth, we realized that cartoonists were able to make inanimate entities engage in animate events including growth. For example, children's books show adult and baby tugboats in New York's harbors. We applied strain and shear to four cartoon-style drawings of Volkswagen Beetles (front and side views, both with and without facial features). The facial features were composed of eyes and eyebrows in the windshield, lines on the hood suggesting a nose, and teeth under the bumper. Strong changes in age were perceived. Strain again had a stronger effect on perceived age than did shear. In addition, inclusion of facial features strengthened the apparent changes in age. Thus, strain was shown to be a transformational invariant for age that applied to a broad class of objects.

We also transformed cartoon drawings of an armchair. The resulting drawings, at least to us, did not seem to vary in apparent age. This showed that there are limits to the set of objects for which strain is the transformational invariant for age. We never did make much progress on establishing these limits. (We also did not ask participants to make age estimates of the armchairs, thereby revealing a bias toward theory confirmation.)

To this point we had shown that strain applied to facial profiles was sufficient to produce changes in perceived age. However, this by itself did not really validate strain as *the* transformation for perceiving growth and age. First, it could well be that the effect of strain on craniofacial growth was merely similar to the effect of some other transformation, one that more accurately captured the actual pattern of physical growth. The perceptual component of our approach to this problem was to have participants view sets of profiles that were generated by strain, transformations similar to strain, and a set traced from longitudinal X-rays. As reported in an article in *Scientific American* (Todd, Mark, Shaw, & Pittenger, 1980), the actual-growth set and the strain set were seen more like growth than any of the other sets. Another component was to compare the effects of strain on skull shape with actual patterns of growth using longitudinal sequences of outline profiles of the skull and mandible of a number of individuals traced from X-rays. As also reported in the *Scientific American* article, strain applied to, for example, the profile of a person at 7 years old was able to match quite closely that person's actual profile at 22 years. Finally, in what might be called the analytic component, Shaw and others went on to study the physics underlying growth. Analyses of the forces that apply to a human head as it grows produced growth equations that were varieties of strain. The details of the history of this work are given in Len Mark's article in this issue of *Ecological Psychology*.

Another problem we faced was that we had shown that the skull grew according to strain, but we had done our perceptual tests on faces, not skulls. This was a problem in that facial skin is not of uniform thickness (the thickness of the lips is not the same as the thickness of the skin on one's forehead). In addition, some skin is not supported by bone (e.g., the nose). In other words, the transformation visible to perceivers is not the one we had physically validated. Shaw and I were not, however, able to make much progress on this important problem.

We also realized that change in shape is not the only effect of aging: skin wrinkles, sags, and coarsens; facial hair develops; and so on. We conducted one study in which age estimates were collected for faces whose shape and degree of skin wrinkling were changed (Mark et al., 1980). Both variables, not surprisingly, influenced perceived age. Another finding was that when the two transformations were combined in unnatural ways, for example, heavy wrinkling on a young-shaped face, between-subjects variability increased. (That increase in variability is a nice example of the consequences of breaking the coordination of transformations, and thereby information, found in natural events.)

HOW WELL DID WE DO?

Bob Shaw's age perception project was not, of course, an ideal set of ecological studies of event perception. In addition to the missing pieces I have already mentioned, we never fully documented the phenomenon we were trying to explain. That is, we never established how well age and growth are perceived in everyday life or how fully individual identity is preserved. Thus, we never knew how much of the variance in age perception is due to shape change and how much to other factors. This is, perhaps, forgivable in that experimental psychology as a field rarely establishes the details of the phenomena its theories purport to explain. It can be argued that theorists should develop explanatory principles that, as need arises, can be used by applied psychologists to solve problems of practical importance. I sometimes think we leave too much to be done by applied psychologists: How well validated is a theory that has not been shown successful in explaining real-life phenomena?

The idea of application leads me to the final thing we did not do: go commercial. Shaw and I talked a number of times about how useful it would be to have a program into which you could put a photograph of a child who had been missing for some years and produce an approximation of that child's present appearance. As I see the results of the aging programs currently in use, I wonder if we could have produced a more accurate one. In any case, it is worth noting that Shaw's commitment to basic research was so powerful that diverting our time into a moneymaking offshoot of the project was never considered very seriously.

In spite of the various tasks left undone, Shaw's project seems to me to constitute an exceptional body of psychological research. I think it is the best set of event perception studies done to date and one of the better sets guided by the ecological approach.

In retrospect, Shaw's choice of the growth of the human face as the event to study was inspired: Facial structure and the changes made by growth are complex but not intractable, faces are of considerable interest to most people (not just experimental psychologists), and face perception is involved in many aspects of everyday life. Subsequent research into event perception has not concerned such rich, interesting events.

Craniofacial growth, as an event, presented us with challenges that psychologists rarely need to face. The underlying mathematics and physics central to most studies of event perception and naive physics (e.g., pendulum motion, collisions, and ballistic motion) had been worked out before psychologists started to study them. (The availability of these analyses was a factor in their selection as events to study.) On the other hand, the mathematics and physics needed to capture the transformational invariants of growth was not at all obvious when the project started. Indeed, these were studied throughout the entire life of the project.

Both during and after my time on the project, Shaw's unusually deep insight into mathematics was crucial to its success. He was able to see into the real heart of the ideas, ones that often are obscured by the details of the symbolism. Having come to the center with a BA in mathematics from the University of Pennsylvania, I was rather pleased with what I took to be my mathematical insight. However, I would spend hours working out some mathematical idea, somewhat by brute force, and then I would report it to Shaw. He would reply along the lines of, "Of course, it couldn't be any other way." Sometimes he would be able to get me to see just why the idea was so obvious to him.

Another notable feature of the project was the thoroughness of both the analysis of the information available to perceivers and of the documentation of the pickup of that information. It is rare to see such a variety of studies used as converging operations on a small number of empirical claims.

Finally, the project had exceptional breadth, involving perception, mathematics, physics, social psychology, art, cartooning, and a little ethology and evolution. The intellectual milieu at the center in the 1970s certainly contributed to the project's scope. However, the truly key factor was the breadth and depth of Bob Shaw's intellectual interests. Although I have known a number of very sharp people, I have never met anyone who knew so much about so many things. Working with him on this project was a long, intellectually rewarding, and occasionally strange, trip.

REFERENCES

Bransford, J. D., & Franks, J. J. (1971). The abstraction of linguistic ideas. *Cognitive Psychology, 2,* 331–356.

Gibson, J. J. (1986). *The ecological approach to visual perception.* Hillsdale, NJ: Lawrence Erlbaum Associates, Inc. (Original work published 1979)

Gibson, J. J., Kaplan, G. A., Reynolds, H. N., & Wheeler, K. (1969). The change from visible to invisible: A study of optical transitions. *Perception & Psychophysics, 5,* 113–116.

Gould, S. J. (1987). Mickey Mouse meets Konrad Lorenz. *Natural History, 88*(5), 30–36.

Heider, F., & Simmel, M. (1944). An experimental study of apparent behavior. *American Journal of Psychology, 57,* 243–259.

Jenkins, J. J., Wald, J., & Pittenger, J. B. (1978). Apprehending pictorial events: An instance of psychological cohesion. In C. Wade Savage (Ed.), *Minnesota studies in the philosophy of science* (Vol. 9, pp. 129–163). Minneapolis, MN: University of Minnesota Press.

Johansson, G. (1973). Visual perception and a model for its analysis. *Perception & Psychophysics, 14,* 201–211.

Lorenz, K. (1943). Die angeborenen Formen Möglicher Erfahrung. [Innate forms of potential experience]. *Zeitschrift für Tierpsychologie, 5,* 235–409.

Mark, L. S., Pittenger, J. B., Hines, H., Carello, C., Shaw, R. E., & Todd, J. T. (1980). Wrinkling and head shape as coordinated sources of age-level information. *Perception & Psychophysics, 27,* 117–124.

Michotte, A. (1963). *The perception of causality.* New York: Basic Books.

Pittenger, J. B., & Shaw. R. E. (1975a). Aging faces as viscal elastic events: Implications for a theory of non-rigid shape perception. *Journal of Experimental Psychology: Human Perception and Performance, 1,* 374–382.

Pittenger, J. B., & Shaw. R. E. (1975b). Perception of relative and absolute age in facial photographs. *Perception & Psychophysics, 18,* 136–143.

Shaw, R. E., McIntyre, M., & Mace, W. (1974). The role of symmetry in event perception. In R. MacLeod & H. Pick, Jr. (Eds.), *Studies in perception: Essays in honor of J. J. Gibson* (pp. 276–310). Ithaca, NY: Cornell University Press.

Thompson, D. W. (1942). *On growth and form.* New York: Dover. (Original work published 1917)

Todd, J. T., Mark, L. S., Shaw, R. E., & Pittenger, J. B. (1980). The perception of human growth. *Scientific American, 242,* 106–114.

ECOLOGICAL PSYCHOLOGY, 17(3 & 4), 161–191
Copyright © 2005, Lawrence Erlbaum Associates, Inc.

Developing Formative Models of Craniofacial Growth and Workplace Design: Personal Reflections on the Work and Influence of Robert E. Shaw

Leonard S. Mark

Department of Psychology and Center for Ergonomic Research
Miami University

In each domain in which Bob Shaw has conducted programmatic research, he has gone to considerable effort to identify and describe the constraints on the event or activity that is the focus of the research. This entails describing the event or activity at a scale appropriate to human perceivers. The first part of this article offers a personal reflection on Bob Shaw's research on the information for craniofacial growth. At the heart of this program, Bob Shaw worked toward a model that captured physical constraints on craniofacial form. In doing so, Shaw extended the method of coordinate transformations developed by D'Arcy Thompson (1917/1992) by using the language of geometric transformations to formalize the changes in craniofacial form that occur over growth. The second part of this article examines how my research with Marvin Dainoff on seated posture at computer workstations and the description of so-called normal work area is indebted to Shaw's constraint-based approach. The challenge of identifying the constraints on events and activities is an important part of the foundation of Gibson's (1979/1986, Part 1) ecological approach to perception. This task is not to be taken lightly.

Consider Herbert Simon's (1981) parable about an ant on a beach:

We watch an ant make his laborious way across a wind- and wave-molded beach. He moves ahead, angles to the right to ease his climb up a steep dunelet, detours around

---

Correspondence should be addressed to Leonard S. Mark, Department of Psychology and Center for Ergonomic Research, Psychology Building, Miami University, Oxford, OH 45056. E-mail: markls@muohio.edu

a pebble, stops to exchange information with a compatriot. Thus, he makes his weaving, halting way back to his home. (p. 63)

Simon asks what is responsible for the complexity of the ant's path? Does it lie in the ant's cognitive and neural processes or in the complexity of environment, that is, the surface of the beach? Simon is unequivocal—the complexity of the ant's behavior is a product of the complexity of its environment. Psychologists sympathetic to the ecological tradition often refer to Simon's parable as pointing to the importance of constraints governing the construction of the terrestrial environment as a starting point for understanding behavior (e.g., Vicente, 1999). What puzzles me is that Simon (1981) takes his answer to mean that little will be accomplished by focusing on adaptive behavior because it is largely determined by the characteristics of the "outer environment and will reveal only a few limiting characteristics of the inner environment—of the physical machinery that enables a person to think" (p. 66).

From an ecological perspective, the parable of the ant motivates a serious examination of the animal's environment—What is there to be perceived? How is the terrestrial environment constructed? What do animals need to do to survive? This enterprise is a daunting task, one that goes to the very heart of an ecological psychologist's commitment to realism—an idea that Robert Shaw clearly understands. I can find no better illustration of this point than a project on the perception of craniofacial growth that Bob Shaw initiated in the early 1970s. To provide a description of the information that underlies craniofacial growth, Bob Shaw had to examine questions fundamental to biology and the study of morphogenesis. The answers could not be found in biology or medical texts because contemporary biology was focusing on growth at the scales of genes and cells, scales that were too microscopic for understanding the emergence of craniofacial form during ontogeny. Rather, a more macroscopic description of craniofacial morphogenesis was needed, the type that had been proposed by the British naturalist D'Arcy Wentworth Thompson (1917/1992) and had long been out of favor among biologists.

The first part of this article examines how Bob Shaw devised such a description of craniofacial growth, building on the ideas from the works of James Gibson and D'Arcy Thompson. Shaw's program was not a minor undertaking. It required imagination to conceive of how something as complex as a growing head could be described by a seemingly simple mathematical transformation, and it demanded perseverance because much of the development of the growth transformation entailed repetitive calculations carried out by hand or using primitive calculators. Bob Shaw's approach flew in the face of ongoing research on craniofacial growth in medicine and dentistry. Yet more than 30 years after Shaw began this project, I find myself with an increasingly greater appreciation for his work in light of its anticipation of recent developments in the study of complex adaptive systems (e.g., Goodwin, 1994). In reflecting over Bob Shaw's achievement, I realize that his approach has shaped and continues to guide my own research at Miami University on affordances and ergonomics. The second section of this article considers these extensions.

JAMES J. GIBSON AND D'ARCY WENTHWORTH THOMPSON

Constraints and the Environment

The classic formulations of the problem of perception began by noting a mismatch between the environment and sensory stimulation. *Constraints* had to be introduced to reduce degrees of freedom and thereby limit the many possible states of affairs in the world that corresponded to the existing pattern of stimulation. Ever since Kepler dissected the eye of a bull and observed the discrepancies between the retinal image and the world, most students of perception, such as Berkeley and von Helmholtz, have looked to mental processes, past experience, learning, and the like as the source of constraints for delimiting the possibilities for what is in the environment.

In 1950 James Gibson began to consider the environment as a source of those constraints, thereby setting up a different basis for resolving the mismatch. Gibson's (1950) "ground theory of perception" was based on lawful constraints governing the construction of the terrestrial environment. As but one example, gravity yokes objects to the ground plane—even the fact that an object rests on the ground (as opposed to floating in space) can be specified by the shadows cast on the ground.[1] By attending to those constraints, Gibson was able to identify invariant relationships specific to properties in the environment and ongoing events. His famous "stick in the field experiment" (Gibson, 1950, p. 183) demonstrated that size constancy did not break down at far distances as had been previously supposed. He identified the horizon-ratio invariant as a source of information for relative size. Later, Gibson (1966, 1979/1986) realized that a serious commitment to this strategy would entail a more thorough reconceptualization of the problem of perception. Perception could no longer be construed as a passive mental process but as an activity involving the detection of lawfully determined information specific to the layout of the environment, events, and what the perceiver is doing (Gibson, 1966).

For Gibson, not only were constraints instrumental in the construction of the terrestrial environment, they were also central to events—structures undergoing a style of change. Kaplan's work on kinetic occlusion (Gibson, Kaplan, Reynolds, &

---

[1]Bob Shaw pointed out to me that human actors first interacted with cartoon characters in the 1945 film *Anchors Aweigh* (Sidney, 1945). In this film Gene Kelly was dancing with Jerry the mouse. To make it appear that the two characters were dancing on the same surface (ground plane), it was necessary for the animators to hand paint in shadows for Jerry's body. If you look carefully at the scene, you can see the shadows "cast" by Jerry's body.

Wheeler, 1969) provides a nice example. When an object moves behind a stationary object, texture on the surface of the moving object is progressively deleted from view, a phenomena that Gibson referred to as kinetic occlusion. The progressive deletion and accretion of texture elements specifies an object going out of view (but not out of existence) and then coming back into view. The existence of multiple surfaces, one passing behind the other, is revealed through this kinetic occlusion, which depends on a pair of lawful constraints, namely, that surfaces are textured and that opaque surfaces can occlude the texture elements of surfaces if the opaque surface is located between the point of observation and another surface (Gibson, 1979/1986).

Just as environmental constraints were central to Gibson's ecological approach to perception, they were also at the heart of D'Arcy Thompson's (1917/1992) treatise on morphogenesis. For Thompson, biological form was constrained by the forces to which it was subjected. Bone remodels itself in response to the magnitude and direction of the stresses to which it has been subjected, an observation that is known as Wolff's law. Thompson's program for understanding morphogenesis was rooted in the identification of constraints on form.

One of Thompson's (1917/1992) most notable and lasting achievements was to develop a method for visualizing the effects of those constraints on global morphology of organisms. His method of coordinate transformations entailed embedding a biological form (a head of a young child) in a grid and taking a related form (the same person at a later time) and deforming the original grid such that common anatomical landmarks (homologous points) on the two heads maintained the same coordinate on the grid. The deformed grid depicted the transformation undergone by the individual as a result of growth and the various forces acting on it. Figure 1 shows an example of Thompson's method of coordinate transformation that allowed the viewer to "see" the effects of the forces acting on the biological structure.

Thompson's (1917/1992) tool for visualizing these morphological changes due to growth was especially important because growth does not entail only a simple increase in size. To maintain the organism's structural and physiological integrity, changes in (Euclidean) shape as well as size must occur. Simply scaling up on the size of a femur (thigh bone), for example, will produce a decidedly weaker supporting structure because the strength of the supporting structure is proportional to the cross-sectional area (w^2), whereas the weight being supported increases with volume (w^3). This is the essence of allometry, which examines changes in shape that accompany an increase in size.

Scales of Analysis

Describing the environment and the events taking place is a daunting task. James Gibson certainly understood this and appreciated the commitment needed to delineate the constraints governing the construction of the terrestrial environ-

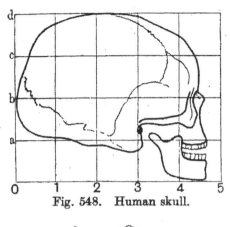

Fig. 548.   Human skull.

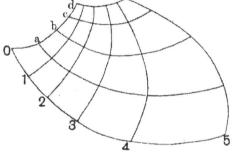

Fig. 549.   Coordinates of chimpanzee's skull, as a projection of
the Cartesian coordinates of Fig. 548.

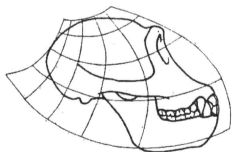

Fig. 550.   Skull of chimpanzee.

FIGURE 1   Illustration of D'Arcy Thompson's method of coordinate transformations. By transforming the grid in which a human's head was embedded (Fig. 548), the shape of the human head was deformed into the head of a chimpanzee (Fig. 550). The deformed grid (Fig. 549) allows the viewer to "see" the transformation. From D'Arcy Thompson, *On Growth and Form*, pp. 1082–1083. Dover Publications, 1992. Used by permission.

ment and the interaction between people and their environment. One has to be impressed with Gibson's (1979/1986, Part 1) meticulous examination of the terrestrial environment in preparation for establishing a lawful basis for information. In doing so Gibson was mindful that the environment and events taking place in the environment can be viewed at different scales of analysis ranging from the molecular all the way to some astrophysical scale. There is no one best scale. Rather, the issue is one of identifying a scale appropriate to each problem. In characterizing the terrestrial environment to which people have adapted, Gibson realized that much of biology and physics of our time was inappropriate for the study of perception. We do not perceive molecules but rather surfaces at a macroscopic scale. Gibson saw the need to ecologize physics and biology such that we can apprehend the lawful regularities at a scale appropriate to human perceivers.

D'Arcy Thompson (1917/1992) also appreciated the task of describing the constraints on growth as it affected the emergence of biological form. Like Gibson, Thompson conveyed an understanding of the limitations of a given scale of analysis. During the early part of the 20th century, contemporary biology was beginning to focus on events at the cellular level. August Weissman had proposed that the germ plasm was the active agent in shaping biological form. Genes were beginning to be recognized as important biological entities. The precursors of the genocentric view (e.g., Dawkins, 1989) that would dominate the latter half of the century were falling into place. But D'Arcy Thompson intuited that macroscopic biological form would not be revealed solely by the activity of genes. More than 50 years later, Thompson's insight has reappeared in various guises in contemporary biology: There is simply not enough information in the genetic code to completely constrain all aspects of biological form (Enlow, 1968). Moreover, there is now ample empirical evidence from the study of simple plants (such as *Acetabularia acetabulum* and slime molds) and unicellular organisms (Paramecium) that genes alone are unable to account for biological form (Goodwin, 1994; Sole & Goodwin, 2000).

In the works of D'Arcy Thompson and James Gibson we see the importance of constraints for determining lawful regularities of abstract events such as growth as well as the layout of the terrestrial environment to which people have adapted. Both men emphasized the importance of adopting an appropriate scale at which to examine the event of interest. And each appealed to a scale of analysis that was somewhat foreign to the science of the day, something akin to surfaces, what I like to call a *macroscopic* scale. However, the links among these themes are not found in D'Arcy Thompson or James Gibson's work, though Gibson (1950) did refer to Thompson's treatise. Rather, it was Bob Shaw who saw these relationships and figured out how they might be used to describe the slow biological event that underlies the perception of growing faces (see Shaw, McIntyre, & Mace, 1974; Shaw & Pittenger, 1977).

DESCRIPTIVE AND FORMATIVE MODELS
FOR STUDYING CRANIOFACIAL GROWTH

As the human head grows, it not only increases in size, but it also changes its shape. A large cranium and a diminutive facial mask characterize the head of the young child. The facial mask, however, grows faster than the cranium, thereby resulting in a marked change in facial proportions. What Shaw set out to do was develop a description of the global remodeling of the craniofacial complex that captures the information for the perception of growth. This information had to be abstract to provide the basis for how a diverse set of heads can be perceived as undergoing the same style of change. The product broke new ground both in the study of event perception and in its applications to the fields of orthodontics and craniofacial surgery. To appreciate how Shaw's work was innovative, especially in the study of craniofacial growth, and how it challenged accepted methods for describing growth, Shaw's formative or constraint-based approach must be contrasted with the traditional descriptive approach that dominated cephalometrics in anthropology and the clinical sciences like dentistry and orthodontics.

In his book on *Cognitive Work Analysis*, Kim Vicente (1999) distinguishes *descriptive* and *formative* approaches[2] (I will use the term *models*) to work analysis. The heart of this distinction is applicable to the description of events such as a growing head. Descriptive models are concerned with describing how an event or activity unfolds from records of actual growth of individuals. Heads of an individual at two different times are compared—the difference between the two heads is taken as growth. In doing so, the resulting descriptions are inclusive of all the constraints specific to the situation, that is, they do not differentiate constraints common to all individuals from those specific to an individual. For this reason descriptive models are unable to cope with the context-conditioned variability inherent to complex systems like growing heads.

Formative (constraint-based) models are less concerned with predicting growth than identifying and modeling constraints on craniofacial form. These models encompass specific conditions rather than an ill-defined set of conditions. Formative models reveal possibilities for what might happen under a specific set of constraints. As such, formative models are well suited for dealing with context-conditioned variability that results from the fact that each individual is subject to a

---

[2]Vicente (1999) refers to descriptive and formative *approaches* when referring to their application to work analysis. A reviewer of this manuscript remarked that I am using Vicente's notions of formative and descriptive approaches, not as a general framework (e.g., ecological approach to perception), but as a method for *implementing* the ecological approach to perceiving and acting. To avoid obscuring Bob Shaw's ecological approach with strategies and tactics for implementing that approach, I am adopting Runeson's (1988) distinction between an approach level and implementation level. Thus, I refer to descriptive and formative *models* rather than approaches.

different set of constraints—this is the very essence of D'Arcy Thompson's approach to morphogenesis.

The classic method for describing growth begins by taking pictures of an individual at various ages and identifying a common set of anatomical landmarks (homologous points) in each picture. From these landmarks, various distances between landmarks, angles, and proportions can be established at each age. "Growth" is taken as the difference between these measures at different ages. The description of growth emerges when these changes are averaged across individuals, thereby producing "norms" that depict the average amount of change in a given dimension from one age to another. This is much the same strategy that psychologists have traditionally used to study the perception of change (cf. Shaw & Pittenger, 1978): Take two static images; identify homologous points in the two images; and superimpose the images. Change is inferred as the difference in the location of homologous points. Because the two approaches are so similar, we should not be surprised to find that they encounter similar difficulties. Shaw and Pittenger (1978) and Todd and Mark (1981) have pointed out that arbitrary choices have to be made pertaining to how different images are superimposed on one another so that the resultant difference depicts the style of change of interest. The resultant description of the underlying event is influenced by those arbitrary decisions.

In his program to construct a description of growth, Bob Shaw rejected the descriptive strategy for many of the same reasons that he rejected it in the context of describing change. With hindsight, however, there was one reason that was probably most important and that guided his efforts to devise a satisfactory alternative. Growth is not the only constraint affecting head shape: Diet, oral habits (e.g., nail biting, thumb sucking), allergies (mouth breathing), and facial trauma have demonstrable effects on craniofacial appearance. By measuring the difference between craniofacial landmarks at two different times, descriptive models necessarily pick up the effects of these nongrowth constraints. Thus a descriptive strategy measures more than growth.

It is evident from Shaw's writings (Shaw et al., 1974; Shaw & Pittenger, 1977; also, Pittenger & Shaw, 1975) and many hours of personal discussions that Bob Shaw was impressed with the insights afforded by D'Arcy Thompson's method of coordinate transformations. In the chapter detailing this method, Thompson provided numerous examples of how his method enabled viewers to "see" the morphological changes that occurred due to growth or the similarities between species. Many of these pictures have been reproduced in a variety of different places. However, I suspect that one particular set of pictures caught Shaw's eye and influenced his initial thinking about how to describe the slow biological event of craniofacial growth. These were the diagrams of dicotyledenous leaves, the Begonia daedalea (Thompson's Fig. 499) and the violet leaf (Thompson's Fig. 501) that are reproduced in Figure 2. Both of these dicotyledenous leaves grow from a fixed point known as a nodal point. Thompson identified two growth vectors—a radial vector that dilates the leaf (increases size) and a tangential vector that effectively varies the rate of dilation around the

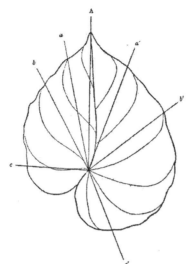

Fig. 499.   *Begonia daedalea.*

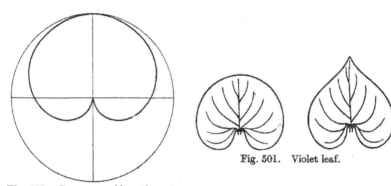

Fig. 501.   Violet leaf.

Fig. 500.   Curve resembling the outline of a reniform leaf: $r = \sin \theta/2$.

FIGURE 2   Picture of *Begonia daedalea* (top) and D'Arcy Thompson's attempt to fit a cardioid
to the outline of a leaf growing from a nodal point. From D' Arcy Thompson, *On Growth and
Form*, p. 1042 and 1045. Dover Publications, 1992.

leaf's perimeter (shearing transformation). Shaw found these forms of interest because the human also appears to grow from a nodal point (Enlow, 1968). The profile
of a human head has many of the characteristics of a dichotyledenous shape—the
rounded cranium, bilateral symmetry around a vertical plane passing through the
ear-hole and a fixed point located at the ear hole around which growth appears to occur. Shaw undoubtedly observed Thompson's Fig. 500, in which a heart-shaped geo-

metric form known as a cardioid was fit to the top half of a circle, thereby revealing the cardioid's similarity to the circumference of the dichotyledenous leaves (Shaw et al., 1974). Had Thompson actually superimposed the cardioid on top of either leaf, the cusp of the cardioid would have roughly coincided with the leaf's nodal point. With this in mind, Shaw attempted to fit a cardioid to the profile of a human skull. Figure 3 shows that the untransformed cardioid, whose cusp was superimposed on the skull's ear-hole, did a reasonable job fitting the inner part of the skull though it was too rounded to fit the outer profile. However, by straining the cardioid, Shaw produced a transformed cardioid that fit the profile of the skull. This strain transformation enabled Shaw to transform the profiles of a 1 year old, 10 year old, and 25 year old into one another. This strain transformation became known as *cardioidal strain*—written in polar coordinates:

$$\theta' = \theta,$$
$$R' = R\,(1 - k\cos\theta) \tag{1}$$

where k is a free parameter that varies the amount of strain. Looking at the equations, we can see both a radial component of growth (the equation $\theta' = \theta$ indicates that each point grows in a straight line radiating from the nodal point) and a tangential component, where the new value of R, that is, R', is a function of both the initial value of R and θ.

FIGURE 3   Shaw transformed a cardioid (small dots) to fit the profile of a human head (large dots) using a strain transformation. Compare to Figure 2. From Shaw, McIntyre, and Mace (1974). Reprinted from *Perception: Essays in Honor of James J. Gibson*, edited by Robert MacLeod and Herbert Pick, Jr. Copyright © 1974 by Cornell University. Used by permission of the publisher, Cornell University Press.

What most people don't appreciate about this exercise is that Bob Shaw transformed the cardioid to fit the skull by hand. That is, he performed the computations using "a pencil on the back of an envelope" and plotted the points manually on graph paper—a true labor of love reflecting his commitment to the approach. Once the cardioidal strain transformation was established, Shaw enlisted the assistance of a computer programmer who was able to apply the transformation to rectangular grids (Shaw & Pittenger, 1977, their Figure 1) and the silhouette profile of a human head (their Figure 2). This took place in the early days of graphics programming when few programmers had meaningful experience with graphics. The difficulties encountered in this initial stage can be seen in Figure 2 of Shaw et al. (1974, p. 306) in which the published heads were unintentionally rotated.

Working with John Pittenger, Bob Shaw now had a description of craniofacial growth and faces produced by the growth transformation that permitted them to examine whether the effects of the transformation were perceived as growth. To compare the effects of the cardioidal strain transformation to those produced by an affine shear transformation that effectively changed the facial angle in a manner consistent with growth, Pittenger and Shaw (1975) asked observers to judge the relative ages of the resultant heads. The outcome of the perceptual judgments was clear cut: The cardioidal strain transformation accounted for over 95% of the variation in age-level judgments in contrast to affine shear, which predicted less than 60% of the variation. Here, then, was a transformation that was modeled after the effects of growth and whose effects were perceived as growth.

Shaw's goal was to devise a transformation that captured the abstract information that specifies the style of change perceived as craniofacial growth. Styles of change such as translating, rotation, bending, stretching, running, walking, or growing can be perceived over a variety of different structures. Thus, it was important to determine that the effects of the cardioidal strain transformation were perceived as growth over a variety of different heads and structures. Mark, Todd, and Shaw (1981) showed that a number of different human heads, including profiles of men and women, could be perceived as growing under cardioidal strain. Pittenger, Shaw, and Mark (1979) took this a step further, demonstrating that the cardioidal strain transformation resulted in the perception of growth when applied to profiles of cartoon animals (their Figure 2) and even inanimate objects—Volkswagen Beetles (their Figure 5). These findings showed the generality of the information produced by the cardioidal strain transformation. During this period Bob Shaw was also engaged in articulating the metatheoretical framework on which a commitment to a critical realism might be grounded (Shaw & Bransford, 1977; Shaw, Turvey, & Mace, 1980). It had to be reassuring for Shaw to see that what we perceive is so closely tied to the actual event—after all, it would be a strange world if what was perceived as growth bore little resemblance to the actual event.

Taking stock of the project to this point, Bob Shaw had devised a mathematical transformation that when applied to a coordinate system would transform the coordinate system and whatever was embedded in that coordinate system. When heads were properly registered and oriented in the coordinate system, the effects of the transformation were perceived as growth. Shaw had taken a step beyond D'Arcy Thompson's (1917/1992) method of coordinate transformations by formalizing the change depicted in the grids using a mathematical transformation.

At the same time, Bob Shaw recognized several important limitations of this growth model. The most obvious limitation of the original transformation was that it did not produce an increase in head size. But for Shaw there was a more important concern: The cardioidal strain transformation was purely descriptive of changes in head shape associated with growth. In devising the transformation, Shaw took craniofacial growth as analogous to the nodal point growth of dicotyledenous leaves. The resulting transformation was sensible in that it captured several notable changes in head shape, including the change in the relative proportions of the facial mask and cranium and the change in the facial angle. But Mark et al. (1981) had also shown that the effects of cardioidal strain were not unique in their ability to produce the appearance of growth. Cardioidal strain was a member of a class of transformations whose effects were perceived to be nearly equivalent to growth. How might one distinguish among members of that group of transformations? This finding made Shaw even more attentive to the fact that the cardioidal strain transformation was not motivated by the physical and biological constraints acting on the craniofacial complex. Shaw understood that D'Arcy Thompson (1917/1992) never intended the grids produced by his method of coordinate transformations to be simply descriptive of morphological change. Rather, their value was to allow observers to "see" the forces acting on the system and to recognize when similar forces shaped different biological forms. Grids showing similar patterns of deformation would reveal the operation of similar constraints across different structures. Said differently, Shaw realized that the existing growth transformation did not capture the biodynamic constraints that shaped the craniofacial complex—the model was not yet formative.

Shaw and his colleagues began looking for dynamic constraints that satisfied two criteria: First, a candidate constraint had to be *universal* in that it had to apply to all instances of growth. Second, the constraint had to act *globally*, that is, over the entire craniofacial complex. This point reminds us that the craniofacial complex can be viewed at various scales—molecular, cellular, histological, and as a macroscopic form. It is at this last scale at which psychologists interested in the perception of craniofacial growth must focus. There are very few constraints other than gravity that satisfy these criteria.

To examine how gravity might affect craniofacial form, we considered a classic problem in hydrostatics: Imagine a spherical tank filled with water (Figure 4). What can we say about the distribution of pressure on the walls of the tank? A hydrostatic analysis indicates that (a) the pressure is continuous over the entire wall of the tank; (b) the magnitude of pressure at any point is a function of the amount of water above that point—thus, it increases as you move from the top to the bottom of the tank; (c) at any point on the wall of the tank the direction of pressure is

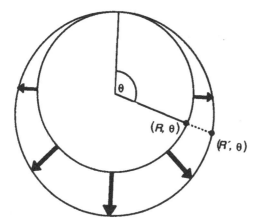

FIGURE 4 Model of a spherical water tank (inner circle) and the pressure distribution inside the tank. The outer circle reflects the form that the tank would assume if it were to remodel in accordance with the direction and amount of pressure from the water inside the tank.

orthogonal to the wall of the tank; and (d) the pressure distribution is bilaterally symmetrical around the vertical axis coincident with the direction of gravity. Recalling Wolff's law, suppose that the walls of the water tank are made of a material that would deform in accordance with the direction and amount of force acting on the system. A pair of equations (written in polar coordinates) describes this transformation:

$$\theta' = \theta,$$
$$R' = R\,[1 + k\,(1 - \cos\theta)] \tag{2}$$

where k refers to a free parameter that determines the overall amount of remodeling. When applied to a human head, this transformation produced an increase in head size as well as head shape (Figure 5). This revised cardioidal strain transformation captured the effects of a gravitational constraint on the craniofacial complex.

As can be seen in Figure 5, the effects of this transformation on a human head looked like growth—people consistently saw the head as growing older. In addition, Todd and Mark (1981) used this transformation to make accurate growth predictions by applying it to the midsagital profiles of X-rays of children to predict what they would look like at a later time. Figure 6 shows examples of these growth predictions. Notice that the revised cardioidal strain predicted both changes in size and shape of the craniofacial complex.

This research was published in the *American Journal of Orthodontics* (Todd & Mark, 1981) and pointed to a potential application of this project. One of the challenges facing orthodontists, plastic oral surgeons, and maxillofacial surgeons

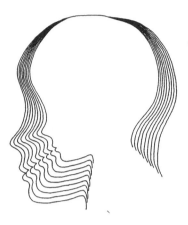

FIGURE 5   Transformed heads produced by applying the revised cardioidal strain transformation (Equation 2) to the innermost profile. Revised cardioidal strain models the changes in head size and shape that are produced by growth. Increasing the amount of the free parameter of the revised cardioidal strain transformation results in an increase in perceived age level.

who treat children with craniofacial disorders and disfigurements was that it was difficult to predict how growth would affect the outcome of their treatment. These clinical specialists have tremendous technical skills—they are able to manipulate every part of the craniofacial complex, both hard and soft tissue. Yet these practitioners were hesitant to operate on children who had not stopped growing because the effects of growth on the immediate treatment outcome were unpredictable, often causing a relapse of the original condition that could be even more difficult to correct. The decision about whether to operate on these children prior to the completion of growth was particularly difficult because children with craniofacial disfigurements face the prospect of going through their formative years with an unattractive visage. What these clinicians lacked was a viable means for predicting the effects of their proposed treatment over the remainder of the child's growth period. This growth transformation had the promise of offering such a predictive tool.

In thinking about this application, Shaw realized that a viable model for predicting craniofacial appearance over the course of the growth period entailed more than accounting for a single constraint. It was necessary to model not only those constraints on craniofacial form that are common to all people but also those specific to each individual. Earlier it was noted that nongrowth constraints such as diet and oral-facial habits like thumb sucking and nail biting could have demonstrable effects on craniofacial form. To accurately predict craniofacial appearance for an individual, each constraint affecting the individual would have to be understood and modeled. This pointed toward a shortcoming of the growth predictions produced by Todd and Mark (1981).

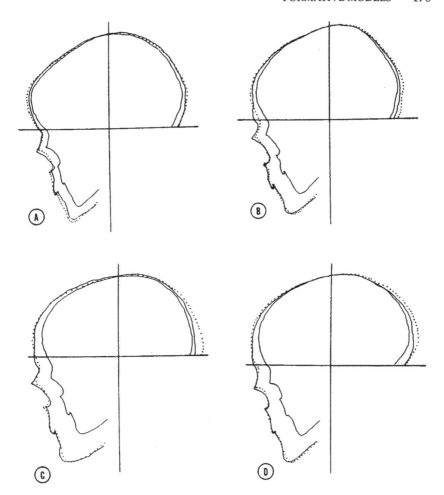

FIGURE 6   Growth predictions produced by revised cardioidal strain transformation to the hard tissue (bone) profile of a young child (innermost solid line). The outermost solid line represents the actual profile of the child at a later age. The dotted line represents the prediction made by transforming the younger profile with revised cardioidal strain. A. Male profile, ages 5.9 and 13.9 years. B. Male profile, ages 6.3 and 19.0 years. C. Male profile, ages 4.3 and 18.6 years. D. Male profile, ages 5.1 and 17.0 years. Reprinted from *American Journal of Orthodontics, 242,* J. T. Todd and L. S. Mark, "Issues Related to the Prediction of Craniofacial Growth," p. 74. © 1981, with permission from the American Association of Orthodontists.

In making their growth predictions, Todd and Mark (1981) began by taking the head of a young child, age 8 years, and used the revised cardioidal strain transformation to predict the child's appearance at some later age, say 15 years. The cardioidal strain transformation should ideally account for the entire difference between the profiles of the child at the two ages. Underlying this strategy for predicting growth lay an important assumption: Craniofacial form is constrained only by the growth potential modeled by cardioidal strain. That is, the strategy for making growth predictions neglected the effects on craniofacial form produced by constraints specific to each individual. Thus, we found ourselves trying to use the growth transformation to predict more than growth. We had still not developed a principled means for modeling the constraints specific to each individual.

Formative Models of Craniofacial Growth

In April 1980, an overview of our work was published in *Scientific American* (Todd, Mark, Shaw, & Pittenger, 1980). Shortly after the article appeared, D. Harvey Jenkins, a retired orthodontist living in Australia, saw the article and arranged to visit with Bob Shaw and his research group. Years earlier at the University of Toronto, Jenkins had developed a method of craniofacial assessment that was remarkably similar to our own work. Because of ill health, he had to abandon his clinical practice and retire to a more favorable climate. It was in those discussions between Harvey Jenkins and Bob Shaw that the basis for a hydrodynamic model of growth emerged.

The revised cardioidal strain transformation resulting from the hydrostatic model could produce only rectilinear growth paths. This is because the transformation is not transitive, meaning that transforming a face at time t_1 to produce a face at a later time, t_2, and then transforming the face at t_2 to produce the face at t_3 is not equivalent to transforming the original face, t_1, to produce the face at t_3. Said differently, the free parameter, k, which determines the amount of change was not transitive—a single transformation of 0.20 was not equivalent to two consecutive transformations of 0.10. This presented an important difficulty for the hydrostatic model because Harvey Jenkins presented us with evidence from his clinical practice that optimal craniofacial growth entails curvilinear trajectories. What we needed to do was transform the hydrostatic model into a hydrodynamic model. In this endeavor, the presence of mathematician Domina Spencer (Moon & Spencer, 1971) at the University of Connecticut was invaluable in showing Bob Shaw how to set up the partial differential equations needed to change from rectilinear to curvilinear coordinates. Carello, Grosofsky, Shaw, Pittenger, and Mark (1989, their Figure 3) presented the resulting coordinate system, which consisted of a tangent-circle geometry in which the curved streamlines represent the growth trajectories and the equipotential curves represent an idealized facial curve at a given time.

Although the hydrodynamic model provided a more defensible method for predicting growth, it was unable to capture the stresses specific to each person. That is, it still predicted "more than growth." The transformation made identical predictions for a pair of identical faces, even though each person might be subject to different forces. This is the reason that Harvey Jenkins's notion of an *archetype* was so important—it provided the means to incorporate potentials other than growth or gravity into the growth model thereby affording the ability to tailor a prediction to the circumstances peculiar to each person.

Jenkins was very fond of a statement that he claimed was from Aristotle: "Each child is his own measuring stick." From my own conversations with Harvey Jenkins, I am convinced that this idea is crucial for understanding what is unique to the archetypal model. In Jenkins's clinical experience, an archetypal face was the product of optimal growth. He developed a method for measuring how closely a face approached its archetype by determining the relationship between a pair of curves that were fit to the craniofacial complex. First, he fit an arc, F, to the facial curve (defined by three anatomical landmarks: nasion, point A, and pogonion on an X-ray). As the face grows, the arc of the circle fit to the facial curve increasingly approximates a straight line; that is, the radius of the circle increases. Jenkins fit a second curve through articulare and the medial bite plane of the upper and lower teeth. Under optimal growth the two curves should intersect at right angles. Any departure from orthogonality was indicative of the effects of additional nonoptimal constraints. For Jenkins, the goal of orthodontic treatment was to restore an orthogonal relationship between these two curves. Jenkins referred to the orthodontic appliance that he used in treatment as a "director" because it functioned to direct the forces affecting craniofacial form to restore the archetypal form. In effect, each face was being measured and evaluated with respect to an intrinsically defined reference system. Treatment for each child was formulated in terms of his or her own unique reference system. Jenkins's ideas about craniofacial measurement were borne out in a study that provided evidence for the relation between perceived facial attractiveness and the distance of the facial profile from its archetype (Carello et al., 1989). Carello et al. show a picture (their Figure 4) of the archetypal model of growth.

With the insights afforded by Jenkins's facial archetype, Bob Shaw's attempt to develop a constraint-based approach to modeling the information for craniofacial growth was realized. His goal was not simply to produce a picture of what the head would eventually look like. Rather, Shaw wanted a method to formally characterize the dynamic constraints (potentials) producing craniofacial change. This captures the invariants responsible for the perception of growth and the various structural properties of faces. In doing so, Bob Shaw was attempting to include the information used by craniofacial experts in their diagnosis and assessment of craniofacial disorders. To realize this aim, Shaw understood that nothing less than a serious commitment to understanding the phenomena surrounding craniofacial growth and morphology would suffice. Bob Shaw's collaboration with Harvey Jenkins resulted in a chapter in a clinical volume on bone growth (Shaw, Mark, Jenkins, & Mingolla, 1983) that presented the hydrodynamic model to practitioners concerned with craniofacial growth in an effort to show why growth models must be grounded in the dynamic potentials (constraints) affecting craniofacial growth and morphology. Reflecting on this work over 20 years later, this chapter anticipated important themes in the contemporary study of dynamic systems as well as some of Bob Shaw's study of intentional dynamics.

I was fortunate to have worked closely with Bob Shaw for almost 8 years. Although the growth project was not the only enterprise that occupied his time, I witnessed the passion and commitment with which he pursued the study of craniofacial growth and the applications of this work to the diagnosis, assessment, and treatment of children with craniofacial deformities. Bob taught himself everything that he could about the human face. He read what artists had to say. We collaborated with a professor of art, Nathan Knobler, who later became dean of the Philadelphia College of Art. Bob read extensively about the biology of growth, learning about growth-related changes in bone, cartilage, soft tissue, and collagen. He also learned about the origins of craniofacial disfigurements and the problems entailed in their treatment. Bob and I even participated in a head–neck anatomy course at the University of Connecticut Medical Center. At the same time, the human side of this work was dear to Bob. I remember that he was very struck by Francis Cooke MacGregor's book, *Transformation and Identity* (1974), which examined the psychosocial consequences of craniofacial disorders. He had an exquisite appreciation for the psychological and social implications of these craniofacial disfigurements for children and adults. It should not be surprising that Bob Shaw could hold his own with biologists, orthodontists, and oral and maxillofacial surgeons, challenging them not only with tough questions but questions that they had not even thought about. At a time when some people thought a single study on a topic would suffice, Bob Shaw was not afraid to develop the expertise needed to attain a deeper understanding of the phenomena of interest, the type of understanding for which Gibson's ecological approach to perceiving and acting called. It was precisely this commitment to examining the constraints underlying the phenomena of interest that I brought with me to Miami University in 1983 when I began to study a different set of problems resulting from the introduction of microcomputers to the workplace.

CONSTRAINTS AND THE DESIGN OF ERGONOMIC WORKSTATIONS

The Problems of Seated Posture and the Design of Ergonomic Chairs

Marvin Dainoff likes to tell a story about how when I arrived at Miami University in 1983 he asked me what Gibson had to say about sitting. To set the context for our collaboration that continues to this day, Marv had just returned to Miami University after a 2-year research appointment at the National Institute for Occupational Safety and Health in which he had conducted research on the occupational stresses associated with working at a video display terminal (Dainoff, 1982). One of

Marv Dainoff's achievements was to conduct a study on the efficacy of ergonomic interventions for computer operators in which he compared the performance of operators working in a best-case and not-so-good-case situation. Dainoff, Fraser, and Taylor (1982) reported a 24% increase in productivity for people working in the best-case workstation compared to their performance in the less optimal workstation. Other findings pointed to the cost effectiveness of ergonomic interventions, notably Spilling, Eitrheim, and Aaras's (1986) study of ergonomic interventions in a German telephone company that documented a return on investment over a 2-year period that exceeded 700%. As a whole, the evidence pointed toward the importance of determining what constitutes appropriate workstation design and working conditions.

This was especially true with respect to ergonomic chairs that would support sitting for prolonged periods because a controversy had erupted among proponents of different seated postures. Most people have encountered the traditional prescription for how to sit when a grade school teacher told us to "sit upright." Figure 7 (top) shows why Mark, Dainoff, Moritz, and Vogele (1991) described an *upright posture* as a cubist position—the trunk was supposed to be at right angles to the thighs, which in turn were at right angles to the lower legs. In the absence of an appropriate backrest, which is technically not needed to maintain an upright posture, the body's weight is centered over two inverted pyramids in the pelvis, the ischial tuberosities. Thus, the buttocks and thighs support the bulk of the body's weight. Over the course of an hour, this can lead to ischemia, a potentially dangerous condition in which blood flow to the buttocks and thighs is restricted. To relieve the discomfort, people typically squirm in their seats or stand up to take a break from their work.

For this reason Grandjean, Hunting, and Pidermann (1983) proposed working in a *backward leaning* posture (Figure 7, bottom left) that was afforded by a backward tilting seat pan and backrest. This would distribute the weight over a greater part of the body—the thighs, buttocks, and back. Grandjean et al. provided evidence that a backward tilt of 15° or more was preferred by computer operators and reduced stress on the lower back. Proponents of the backward tilting posture noted that many people spontaneously adopt a backward leaning slouch, even when the chair does not afford proper seat pan and backrest adjustments. Slouching, however, was not desirable because it promoted a spinal kyphosis (outward curve of the lumbar spine that places excessive pressure on the spinal discs). To avoid this slouch, Grandjean et al. argued that the chair should afford a spinal lordosis (inward curve of the lumbar spine) by offering backrests that tilt backward and lumbar supports that are sculpted to fit the spine. Thus, Grandjean et al. had offered a normative prescription for how people should sit; much of the evidence in support of their recommendation was based on descriptions of how people actually prefer to sit.

This backward leaning alternative to the upright posture was challenged by Mandel (1981) who offered a different prescription for how people should sit, a *for-

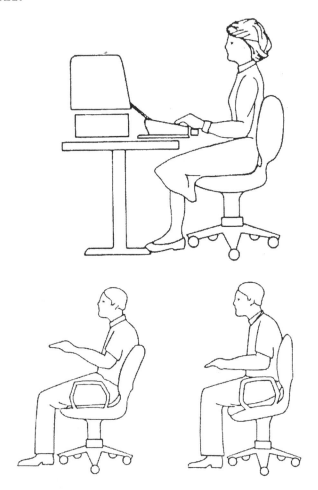

FIGURE 7   Upright posture (top), backward leaning (bottom left), and forward leaning (bottom right) working postures. From "An Ecological Framework for Ergonomic Research and Design" by L. S. Mark, M. J. Dainoff, R. Moritz, and D. Vogele in *Cognition and the Symbolic Processes: Applied and Ecological Perspectives* (p. 480) by R. R. Hoffman & D. S. Palermo (Eds.). Copyright © 1991 by Lawrence Erlbaum Associates, Inc. Reprinted with permission.

ward leaning posture (Figure 7, bottom right) that was supported by a forward tilting seat pan and backrest. This allowed the legs to bear more of the weight, thus reducing the stress on the buttocks and thighs. Mandel further argued that the forward leaning posture promoted the desired spinal lordosis more effectively than the other seated postures. Like Grandjean et al. (1983), Mandel (1981) offered similar empirical evidence in support of his prescription. (In the early 1980s one of the popular chairs among office workers and computer users was the kneeling chair, which promoted a forward leaning seated posture.)

It is at this point that I arrived at Miami University and Marv Dainoff posed his question about what Gibson would say about sitting. Marv was hoping that there was something in the ecological approach that might offer a rationale for resolving these conflicting proposals. Without realizing it at the time, my experience working on the growth project with Bob Shaw led our research group to examine the ecology of sitting for the purpose of identifying the constraints on the act of sitting.

One of the constraints we considered was the difficulty in maintaining a single seated posture for a long period of time without running the risk of ischemia. Watching some of Marv Dainoff's videotapes of people sitting over the course of an 8-hr workday convinced us that sitting was not a static posture. Over the course of an hour, people moved around quite a bit (Mark, Vogele, & Dainoff, 1985). Our analyses of Dainoff's videotapes echoed the findings of a descriptive study by Branton (1969), who filmed people sitting on the hard benches of passenger cars. His time-lapse photography revealed that over the course of roughly 25 min, passengers progressively slumped on the seat—the chair seemingly ejected the passenger—until the passengers righted their posture and began the process all over again. (As university professors, we saw illustration of Branton's findings in our classes, where students slide out of their fixed classroom chairs at similar intervals and then right their posture only to begin the process again.) It seemed that movement was essential for maintaining a seated posture for a prolonged period of time.

We also observed that there was much to recommend each of the prescribed postures. With proper support from the chair, each posture can promote the spinal lordosis that was regarded to be desirable in preventing compression of spinal discs. Each posture was regarded to be comfortable, at least for a short period of time. We also noticed that each posture distributed body weight over different parts of the body. And, finally, we observed that each posture had advantages and disadvantages over the other postures in terms of performing specific tasks.

It occurred to me that the field was asking the wrong question. The issue was *not* to identify the optimal posture. The constraints on sitting dictated that a single fixed posture could not be maintained for a prolonged period. Rather, the issue was to identify postures that satisfy the requirements of the particular task being performed such that people can work safely and productively. In this context, upright, backward, and forward leaning postures may be viewed as complementing one another rather than mutually exclusive alternatives. We quickly came to understand that each of these postures support different activities, that is, each satisfies different task constraints. For example, a forward leaning posture is well suited for copy-intensive, data-entry tasks in which the computer operator has to view hard copy with relatively small letters. This posture places the head closer to the text, thus making it easier to see. In contrast, the backward leaning posture does not support the demands of an entry task, especially for older workers, because the eyes are too far from the copy. But a backward leaning posture does afford screen-intensive editing tasks because the screen characters are relatively large. For operators whose jobs permit them to alternate between screen- and copy-intensive tasks, moving between postures not only would allow them to satisfy the task constraints, but it also encourages movement that is necessary to sit for prolonged periods. Dainoff and Mark (1987) demonstrated the efficacy of this approach in a series of experiments in our lab.

Today, it is generally accepted among ergonomists that there is not a single optimal posture. Rather, ergonomists recognize that upright, forward, and backward leaning postures satisfy different task constraints. By identifying organismic and task constraints on the act of sitting for prolonged periods, we were able to show that multiple postures are required to sit for a prolonged period. A good ergonomic chair must not only afford those working postures but also the capability to move from one posture to another.

As I reflect on my 21-year collaboration with Marv Dainoff, I am most proud of our role in persuading the ergonomic community that a single seated posture will not suffice for people working at computer terminals for prolonged periods of time. Our insights about this problem were directly attributable to our focus on the constraints governing seated posture. With the benefit of hindsight, it is easy to see Bob Shaw's hand on this project (Dainoff, Mark, & Gardner, 1999).

Constructing a Model of Work Area

As part of our collaboration, Marv Dainoff and I also considered the system integration problem—how the components of a computer workstation can be integrated to facilitate the work being performed. The concept of work area was originally proposed by Maynard (1934) in an attempt to define an area around the worker in which the amount of movement (and consequently energy expenditure) could be kept to a minimum. Maynard's intention was to delimit regions in which work could be performed comfortably and efficiently. *Normal work area* was defined as an area that workers act in using movement of the fingers, wrist, and forearm. Maximum work area included movements of the entire arm. Following Maynard, other normative prescriptions for work area (e.g., Chapanis, Garner, & Morgan, 1945; Farley, 1955; Squires, 1959) have been offered based on the assumption that a seated worker maintains a fixed upright working posture in which a vertical upper torso is perpendicular to the upper legs, which in turn are perpendicular to the lower legs. Consider Squires's approach: By pivoting the right upper arm around the shoulder and the lower arm around the elbow, Squires produced the outline of a work area depicted in Figure 8. He was able to derive a pair of equations for the coordinates of any point on this distal boundary (PQ), marking the outer limit of the work area. Although Squires did not show his derivation, Hyeg Joo Choi and Chull Park (Choi, Mark, Dainoff, & Park, in press) reconstructed this proof. Squires's model of normal work area provided the foundation for later models of normal work area (Das & Behara, 1995; Das & Grady, 1983a, 1983b; Konz & Goel, 1969) and is still a staple of many human factors texts.

Body Median

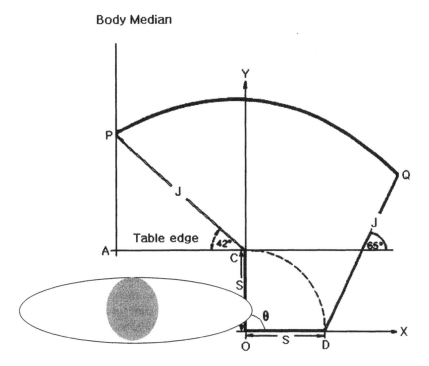

FIGURE 8   Squires's model of normal work area was constructed by rotating the upper arm, S, around the shoulder, O, and having the forearm, J, rotate around the elbow, C. Arc P-Q shows the distal boundary of the derived normal work area. Drawing by Hyeg Joo Choi.

This proof, however, also revealed a curious mistake in Squires's original article. Squires (1959) indicated that the curve of the distal boundary was actually a prolate epicycloid. Choi et al. (in press) proved that the form was actually a hypertrochoid. What is interesting is that prolate epicycloids and hypertrochoids are both related to the cardioid that Bob Shaw worked with in devising the growth transformation. Each of these geometric forms can be constructed by rotating one circle around the circumference of another circle. If the diameters of the two circles are equal, the path traced out by a point on the circumference of the moving circle will form a cardioid. By varying the relative diameters of the two circles and whether the point is on the circumference of the moving circle or on a line extending from the center of the moving circle, different forms can be created, including hypertrochoids and prolate epicycloids. The interested reader might consult the following Web site to explore this relationship in more detail, http://www.cut-the-knot.org/ctk/Cardi.shtml.

When I first encountered Squires's contention that the distal boundary of his normal work area was a prolate epicycloid, I considered the possibility that there might be a deep underlying relation between the working area problem and Shaw's work on growth. I was quite familiar with the work of Peter S. Stevens (1974), who showed many examples of how similar patterns in nature, often at vastly different scales, reflected common underlying dynamic constraints. However, as I studied Squires's model and those related to it, I concluded that the similarity of the forms in Squires's normal working area and Shaw's growth models was mere coincidence because Squires's model was based on unrealistic constraints regarding how people actually reach. Squires assumed workers maintain a fixed upright working posture with only the arms moving around the shoulder. When performing manual work within the normal working area (e.g., part assembly, pick–place, writing, or typing), visual requirements of the task may necessitate tilting the head (and sometimes moving the eyes closer to the objects being manipulated) so that the objects are in the worker's field of view and crucial details can be seen clearly. Because the boundaries of the normal working area are so close to the worker, the worker's head may have to be tilted downward to such an extreme that neck strain would result if that work posture has to be maintained. To reduce the amount of head tilt, a worker might try leaning forward, thereby increasing the distance of the boundaries of the normal working area (because the shoulders have moved forward) and the angle at the elbow (because the shoulder has been lowered and thus the forearm has to be raised in order for the hand to reach the table surface). This situation reveals the interconnectedness among the derived normal working area, body posture, and head tilt required to satisfy the visual requirements of the task. The problem of describing the boundaries of normal working area is further complicated by the fact that an upright posture is difficult to maintain for extended periods (Dainoff & Mark, 1987). As discussed earlier, frequent postural changes are necessary to prevent ischemia and other discomforts and to avoid lower back pain (McGill, 2002). In addition, when reaching, people typically either lean forward or rotate their torso to extend the shoulder of their reach arm (Gardner, Mark, Ward, & Edkins, 2001; Mark et al., 1997). Thus, the "ideal" of a prescribed normal working area based on a single starting posture is flawed from the outset because it fails to take into account constraints on how people reach. Work area is constrained by the worker's posture, the worker's body scale, and biodynamic capabilities, as well as the position of the work surface and tools needed to perform the job. This begs a fundamental question: On what basis should the normal work area be established? Research on how people reach has identified some fundamental constraints on reaching that shed light on this question.

Toward a Formative Model of Normal Work Area

Gardner et al. (2001) offered taxonomy of the macroscopic reach actions used as a function of reach distance (Figure 9). At close distances, the person might reach moving only the arm, an *arm-only reach*. (The arm movements used by Farley, 1955; Squires, 1959; and Chapanis et al., 1945, to construct their normal and maximum work areas reflect arm-only reaches.) At somewhat farther distances people

| Arm-only | Arm-and Shoulder | Arm-and Torso | Partial Standing | Full Standing |

FIGURE 9   An illustsration of the taxonomy of reach actions developed by Gardner et al. (2001).

must introduce other parts of the body to reach the object. Sometimes this is accomplished by rotating the upper torso to extend the shoulder toward the target, an *arm-and-shoulder* reach. On other occasions, the person may also lean forward, an *arm-and-torso* reach. And there is another critical boundary beyond which a seated arm-and-torso reach will no longer suffice, and the person will have to stand, first using a *partial standing* reach similar to a crouch and at farther distances, a *full- standing* reach.

The reach mode used is determined by a variety of constraints pertaining to the worker (organism), the environment, and the task (cf. Newell, 1986). Among the environmental constraints are the reach distance (D) and the size (L) and weight (W) of objects being reached for. Organismic (worker) constraints are determinants of the actor's capabilities and include the relevant aspects of the actor's body scale (b; e.g., arm length) and the actor's strength (s). Task constraints (T) might include specific demands for postural stability and visual requirements involved in performing a task. For example, to thread a 2-mm bead with a needle, the requisite reach action will require the actor to move his or her head close to the bead to see the hole and maintain a stable position to thread the needle (Gardner et al., 2001). The challenge facing researchers is to understand how environmental and task constraints are related to organismic constraints in determining the choice of a macroscopic reach mode in a particular situation.

Each reach mode has its own absolute critical boundary beyond which it can no longer achieve the goal. Thus, people have to scale the reach distance with respect to the limits of their reach capabilities. Research in our lab has also revealed that transitions between reach modes as a function of scaling up on environmental constraints such as distance rarely occurs at the absolute limit of a person's capability (absolute critical boundary) for performing a particular reach mode (Gardner et al., 2001; Mark et al., 1997). Rather, it typically occurs at distances closer than the absolute critical boundary; what Mark (1995) referred to as the preferred critical boundary.

Normative approaches to defining work area are largely grounded in a single organismic constraint—body scale. Indeed, the research on reaching that we have considered to this point, although identifying the roles of organismic and task constraints, still focuses primarily on environmental constraints, specifically distance as a determinant of reach mode. Inasmuch as reach modes are constrained by various combinations of environmental, task, and organismic constraints, it behooves students of formative approaches to develop methods for showing how these constraints can be integrated to determine the reach mode. Toward this goal, Cesari and Newell (1999) have offered a methodology for how multiple constraints might be integrated to study the role of object size and mass in determining the grip used to pick up an object. Choi and Mark (2004) adapted this method to determine the role of environment constraints (object weight, distance) and organismic constraints (actor's size, flexibility, and strength) for determining reach mode. Choi and Mark (2004) had participants pick up containers of five different weights each placed at 10 different distances. Reach distances were scaled with respect to each individual's maximum-seated reach distance. Each weight–distance combination was picked up 10 times in random order. This enabled us to determine a preferred reach mode for each weight–distance combination for each of six men and six women, as well as a collective preference for each gender and for both genders. We also collected a measure of each participant's strength. The average strength measure for each gender was then used to rescale object weight such that weight was now expressed as a dimensionless number (weight in Newtons divided by strength in Newtons). A discriminant analysis using the combined data for both genders revealed that a single discriminant function could predict in excess of 91% of the reach modes used. Figure 10 shows these data in which discriminant functions with a common slope of −36 are fit. The finding that transition lines with a common slope could so accurately predict the reach mode used indicates that this space reveals geometric and dynamic relations that are common to both men and women. As such the *regime space* depicted in Figure 10 reveals how distance (scaled with respect to people's action capabilities) and weight (scaled with respect to strength) constrain the reach actions used by men and women.

Based on Cesari and Newell's (1999) dimensional analysis, Choi and Mark (2004) devised the following equation to describe the transition lines:

$$\ln (W/S) = \beta_0 - 36 \ln D \qquad (3)$$

where β_0 refers to the Y intercept, W refers to the object weight in Newtons, S refers to strength in Newtons, D refers to distance scaled in terms of each participant's maximum seated reach distance, and −36 is the slope obtained from the discriminant analysis. From this we can define a variable K, such that:

$$K = \ln D + [\ln (W/S) / 36] \qquad (4)$$

Choi and Mark (2004) also found that the transition between a pair of reach modes occurs at common values of K for both men and women. Different transitions occur at different values of K. K is a function of object distance, object weight, the ac-

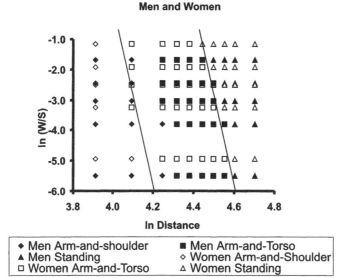

Men and Women

FIGURE 10   The preferred macroscopic reach mode for each reach distance–object weight combination for both men (filled symbols) and women (unfilled symbols). Reach distance is expressed intrinsically in terms of the absolute critical boundary for seated (arm-and-torso) reaches. Object weight is also expressed in intrinsic units of the mean strength for men and women. Both axes show the natural logarithms of these measures. Parallel lines (slope = –35) obtained from the discriminant analysis were drawn to demarcate regions in which each reach mode was preferred. Reprinted from *Human Movement Science*, Volume 23, Hyeg Joo Choi and Leonard S. Mark, Scaling Affordances for Human Reach Actions (2004) with permission of Elsevier.

tor's strength and body scale, and relevant biodynamic capabilities. As such, K captures the relation among these determinants of reach mode used. In short, Figure 10 and Equation 4 capture the effects of environmental, organismic, and task constraints on the macroscopic reach act.

Figure 10 may be construed as part of a formative model of working area. Unlike Squires's (1959) model, it does not provide a simple metric picture of reach area that is independent of reach dynamics; rather, it identifies how various environmental, organismic, and task constraints determine the reach mode used. The data provided in Figure 10 show how reach distance and object weight constrain reach mode. In contrast to normative models, like Squires's, which are derived from idealized assumptions about how people should reach, our formative model is based on how people actually reach—one might think of it as *performance based* because work area boundaries are established by the location of the preferred critical boundaries between reach modes (Choi, Mark, Dainoff, & Harvey, 2003). Admittedly, the information provided in Figure 10 is limited to a single direction. However, it would be a relatively straightforward process to collect similar performance-based reach measures for other reach directions to construct a two dimensional work area (e.g., Choi et al., 2003).

To summarize, Cesari and Newell (1999) and Choi and Mark (2004) have developed a methodology for dealing with the constraints that determine the macroscopic actions that a diverse group of people will use under a variety of circumstances. Studies of the critical boundaries for affordances have often considered only a single constraint. This methodology offers the possibility of examining the task, organismic, and environmental constraints that determine the location of these critical boundaries.

FINAL REFLECTIONS: IS IT PSYCHOLOGY YET?

John Pittenger, Jim Todd, and I spent countless hours with Bob Shaw working on how to present our findings on the perception of growing faces. Invariably, someone would say something to the effect, "What you have done is very interesting, but why is it psychology?" The question came from philosophers, orthodontists, oral surgeons, anthropologists, but most often from other psychologists. The fact that so many psychologists have posed the question probably reflects some of the fundamental differences between ecological psychology and more traditional cognitive approaches. Before asking questions about *how* perception occurs and the events that transpire in the nervous system (process description), the ecological approach demands that we consider *what* there is to be perceived and what animals need to know about (state description). Bob Shaw appreciated this point in the work of James Gibson. We need to consider even what people actually perceive—just because we can ask people to make judgments about a particular dimension does not mean that it is something for which their perceptual skills are well adapted. Sadly, psychologists have often taken the stimulus for perception for granted. Finding it impoverished relative to what they believe people know, students of perception are then faced with the challenge of explaining how the percept is constructed from impoverished snippets of the world.

A colleague at Miami University, Ray White, a cognitive psychologist, once suggested to me that the fundamental task of psychology is to search for the stimulus for behavior. Forgetting any objections that Gibson might raise regarding the use of the terms *stimulus* or *behavior*, I think Ray White has a good point. But in agreeing, I also assert that we must not be glib in our attempt to characterize the environment or take for granted the information available for prospective actors. My reading of Herbert Simon's (1981) *The Sciences of the Artificial* is that Simon recognized the environment as a critical constraint on behavior but underestimated the challenges involved in identifying environmental constraints. This is an awesome task, as Gibson (1979/1986, Part 1) showed us in the examination of the environment to be perceived. Similarly, Bob Shaw's commitment to ecological realism demands a serious examination of the lawful constraints that govern the events and activities around us. It knows no disciplinary bounds, but at the same time analyses from other sciences cannot be accepted uncritically. To identify the lawful constraints shaping the events that are perceived entails perseverance and tenaciousness. It involves not only studying the event-domain from the perspective of the disciplines needed to characterize the relevant constraints but also characterizing the events at a scale appropriate to perception. Such an existential commitment entails many activities that do not fall within the realm of what is usually thought to be the province of psychology. But these are activities that an ecological psychologist must carry out in service of describing the constraints on events and information.

There is another answer to the question of why the work on craniofacial is psychology. Simply put, it is not psychology. It is a good problem; it is good science; it has applications from which people might benefit. In *The Dreams of Reason*, Heinz Pagels (1988) observed that the so-called disciplinary boundaries between fields are very much a product of an archaic classification system perpetuated by universities that insist on maintaining departments of biology, physics, psychology, sociology, etc. Many contemporary problems fall across these traditional boundaries. This is why the enterprise of cognitive science includes philosophers, linguists, engineers, computer scientists, and neuroscientists, as well as psychologists. The study of complex systems similarly cuts across disciplinary lines. This makes our work difficult and poses many challenges. But, as I learned from Bob Shaw, it makes our work fun.

ACKNOWLEDGMENTS

Research and preparation of this manuscript was supported by a grant from the Office of Research and Scholarship at Miami University. The author is grateful to Hyeg Joo Choi, Charles Mark, and Marvin Dainoff for discussions about the issues raised in this article.

REFERENCES

Branton, P. (1969). Behaviour, body mechanics, and discomfort. *Ergonomics 12*, 316–327.

Carello, C., Grosofsky, A., Shaw, R. E., Pittenger, J. B., & Mark, L. S. (1989). Attractiveness of facial profiles is a function of distance from archetype. *Ecological Psychology, 1*, 227–252.

Cesari, P., & Newell, K. M. (1999). The scaling of human grip configuration. *Journal of Experimental Psychology: Human Perception and Performance, 25*, 927–935.

Chapanis, A., Garner, W. R., & Morgan, C. T. (1945). *Applied experimental psychology*. New York: Wiley.

Choi, H. J., & Mark, L. S. (2004). Scaling affordances for human reach actions. *Human Movement Science, 23*, 785–806.

Choi, H. J., Mark, L. S., Dainoff, M. J., & Park, C. (in press). Normative, descriptive and formative approaches to describing work area. *Theoretical Issues in Ergonomic Science*.

Choi, H. J., Mark, L. S., Dainoff, M. J., & Harvey, T. M. (2003, August). *A performance based model of normal working area*. Paper presented at the annual meeting of the International Ergonomics Association, Seoul, Korea.

Dainoff, M. J. (1982). Occupational stress factors in VDT operation: A review of empirical literature. *Behaviour, and Information Technology, 1*, 141–176.

Dainoff, M. J., Fraser, L., & Taylor, B. J. (1982). Visual, musculoskeletal, and performance differences between good and poor VDT workstations. *Proceedings of the Human Factors Society 26th Annual Meeting, 26,* 318–321.

Dainoff, M. J., & Mark, L. S. (1987). Task and the adjustment of ergonomic furniture. In B. Knave & P.-G. Wideback (Eds.), *Work with display units* (pp. 294–302). Amsterdam: North-Holland.

Dainoff, M. J., Mark, L. S., & Gardner, D. L. (1999). Scaling problems in the design of work spaces for human use. In P. A. Hancock (Ed.), *Human performance and ergonomics* (pp. 265–290). San Diego, CA: Academic.

Das, B., & Behara, D. N. (1995). Determination of the normal horizontal working area: A new model and method. *Ergonomics, 38,* 734–748.

Das, B., & Grady, R. M. (1983a). Industrial workplace layout design: An application of engineering anthropometry. *Ergonomics, 26,* 433–447.

Das, B., & Grady, R. M. (1983b). The normal working area in the horizontal plane: A comparative analysis between Farley's and Squires' concept. *Ergonomics, 26,* 449–459.

Dawkins, R. (1989). *The selfish gene.* New York: Oxford University Press.

Enlow, D. (1968). *The human face: An account of the postnatal growth and development of the craniofacial skeleton.* New York: Harper & Row.

Farley, R. R. (1955). Some principles of methods and motion study as used in development work. *General Motors Engineering Journal, 2,* 20–25.

Gardner, D. L., Mark, L. S., Ward, J. A., & Edkins, H. (2001). How do task characteristics affect the transitions between seated and standing reaches? *Ecological Psychology, 13,* 245–274.

Gibson, J. J. (1950). *The perception of the visual world.* Boston: Houghton-Mifflin.

Gibson, J. J. (1966). *The senses considered as perceptual systems.* Boston: Houghton-Mifflin.

Gibson, J. J. (1986). *The ecological approach to visual perception.* Hillsdale, NJ: Lawrence Erlbaum Associates, Inc. (Original work published 1979)

Gibson, J. J., Kaplan, G. A., Reynolds, H. N., & Wheeler, K. (1969). The change from visible to invisible: A study of optical transitions. *Perception & Psychophysics, 5,* 113–116.

Goodwin, B. (1994). *How the leopard changed its spots: The evolution of complexity.* New York: Scribner's.

Grandjean, E., Hunting, W., & Pidermann, M. (1983). VDT workstation design: Preferred settings and their effects. *Human Factors, 25,* 161–175.

Konz, S., & Goel, S. C. (1969). The shape of the normal working area in the horizontal plane. *American Institute of Industrial Engineers Transaction, 1,* 70–73.

MacGregor, F. M. C. (1974). *Transformation and identity: The face and plastic surgery.* New York: Quadrangle.

Mandel, A. C. (1981). The seated man (Homo Sedans), the seated work position, theory and practice. *Applied Ergonomics, 12,* 19–26.

Mark, L. S. (1995). Perceiving the preferred critical boundary for an affordance. In R. Bootsma & B. Bardy (Eds.), *Studies in perception and action III* (pp. 183–186). Hillsdale, NJ: Lawrence Erlbaum Associates, Inc.

Mark, L. S., Dainoff, M. J., Moritz, R., & Vogele, D. (1991). An ecological framework for ergonomic research and design. In R. R. Hoffmann & D. Palermo (Eds.), *Cognition and the symbolic processes* (Vol. 3). Hillsdale NJ: Lawrence Erlbaum Associates, Inc.

Mark, L. S., Nemeth, K., Gardner, D., Dainoff, M. J., Paasche, J. C., Duffy, M., & Grandt, K. (1997). Postural dynamics and the preferred critical boundary for visually-guided reaching. *Journal of Experimental Psychology: Human Perception and Performance, 23,* 1–15.

Mark, L. S., Todd, J. T., & Shaw, R. E. (1981). The perception of growth: A geometric analysis of how different styles of change are distinguished. *Journal of Experimental Psychology: Human Perception and Performance, 7,* 355–368.

Mark, L. S., Vogele, D. C, & Dainoff, M. J. (1985). Measuring movement at ergonomic workstations. In R. E. Eberts of C. G. Eberts (Eds.), *Trends in Ergonomics/Human factors II* (pp. 431–438). Amsterdam: Elsevier.

Maynard, H. B. (1934). Workplace layouts that save time, effort and money. *Iron Age, 134,* 28–30.

McGill, S. (2002). *Low back disorders: Evidence-based prevention and rehabilitation.* Champaign, IL: Human Kinetics.

Moon, P., & Spencer, D. E. (1971). *Field theory handbook.* New York: Springer-Verlag.

Newell, K. M. (1986). Constraints on the development of coordination. In M. G. Wade & H. T. A. Whiting (Eds.), *Motor development in children: Aspects of coordination and control* (pp. 232–256). Boston: Martinus Nijhoff.

Pagels, H. R. (1988). *The dreams of reason: The computer and the rise of the sciences of complexity.* New York: Simon & Schuster.

Pittenger, J. B., & Shaw, R. E. (1975). Aging faces as viscal elastic events. Implications for a theory of nonrigid shape perception. *Journal of Experiemental Psychology: Human Perception and Performance, 1,* 374–382.

Pittenger, J. B., Shaw, R. E., & Mark, L. S. (1979). Perceptual information for the age-level of faces as a higher-order invariant of growth. *Journal of Experimental Psychology: Human Perception and Performance, 5,* 478–493.

Runeson, S. (1988). The distorted room illusion, equivalent configurations, and the specificity of static optic arrays. *Journal of Experimental Pschology: Human Perception and Performance, 14,* 295–304.

Shaw, R. E., & Bransford, J. (1977). Introduction: Psychological approaches to the problem of knowledge. In R. E. Shaw & J. Bransford (Eds.), *Perceiving, acting and knowing* (pp. 1–39). Hillsdale, NJ: Lawrence Erlbaum Associates, Inc.

Shaw, R. E., Mark, L. S., Jenkins, D. H., & Mingolla, E. (1983). A dynamic geometry for predicting growth of gross craniofacial morphology. In A. Dixon & B. Sarnat (Eds.), *Factors and mechanisms in bone growth* New York: Liss.

Shaw, R. E., McIntyre, M., & Mace, W. (1974). The role of symmetry in event perception. In R. MacLeod & H. Pick, Jr. (Eds.), *Studies in perception: Essays in honor of J. J. Gibson* (pp. 276–310). Ithaca, NY: Cornell University Press.

Shaw, R. E., & Pittenger, J. B. (1977). Perceiving the face of changing in changing faces. In R. E. Shaw & J. Bransford (Eds.), *Perceiving, acting and knowing* (pp. 103–132). Hillsdale, NJ: Lawrence Erlbaum Associates, Inc.

Shaw, R. E., & Pittenger, J. B. (1978). On perceiving change. In H. Pick & E. Saltzman (Eds.), *Modes of perceiving and processing information* (pp. 187–204). Hillsdale, NJ: Lawrence Erlbaum Associates, Inc.

Shaw, R. E., Turvey, M. T., & Mace, W. M. (1980). Ecological psychology: The consequences of a commitment to realism. In W. Weimer & D. Palermo (Eds.), *Cognition and the symbolic processes* (Vol. 2, pp. 159–226). Hillsdale, NJ: Lawrence Erlbaum Associates, Inc.

Sidney, G. (Director). (1945). *Anchors aweigh* [Motion picture]. United States: MGM.

Simon, H. A. (1981). *The sciences of the artificial* (2nd ed.). Cambridge, MA: MIT Press.

Sole, R., & Goodwin, B. (2000). *Signs of life.* New York: Basic Books.

Spilling, S., Eitrheim, J., & Aaras, A. (1986). Cost benefit analysis of work environment investment at STK's telephone plan at Kongsvinger. In N. Corlett, J. Wilson, & I. Manenica (Eds.), *The ergonomics of working postures* (pp. 380–397). London: Taylor & Francis.

Squires, P. C. (1959). Proposed shape of normal work area. *Engineering & Industrial Psychology, 1,* 12–17.

Stevens, P. S. (1974). *Patterns in nature.* Boston: Little, Brown.

Thompson, D. W. (1992). *On growth and form.* New York: Dover. (Original work published 1917)

Todd, J. T., & Mark, L. S. (1981). Issues related to the prediction of craniofacial growth. *American Journal of Orthodontics, 79,* 63–80.

Todd, J. T., Mark, L. S., Shaw, R. E., & Pittenger, J. B. (1980). The perception of human growth. *Scientific American, 242,* 106–114.

Vicente, K. J. (1999). *Cognitive work analysis: Toward safe, productive and healthy computer-based work.* Mahwah, NJ: Lawrence Erlbaum Associates, Inc.

ECOLOGICAL PSYCHOLOGY, 17(3 & 4), 193–204
Copyright © 2005, Lawrence Erlbaum Associates, Inc.

Allometry and Space Perception: Compression of Optical Ground Texture Yields Decreasing Ability to Resolve Differences in Spatial Scale

Geoffrey P. Bingham

Department of Psychology
Indiana University

Robert E. Shaw and colleagues showed that allometric variations in biological forms provide visual information about the spatial and temporal scale of biological objects (Mark, Todd, & Shaw, 1981; Pittenger & Shaw, 1975a, 1975b; Pittenger, Shaw, & Mark, 1979; Pittenger & Todd, 1983; Shaw, Mark, Jenkins, & Mingolla, 1982; Shaw & Pittenger, 1977, 1978). In these studies, form changes due to growth of the human head and body were investigated. Subsequently, Bingham (1993a, 1993b) extended these ideas to plant growth and tree perception. Using extant models of tree growth and morphology, 2 allometric relations were simulated. One determined the thickness of tree branches and the other determined their numerocity. The investigations showed that the resulting tree forms could be used by observers to judge tree size. Trees appearing in the context of a ground texture gradient conferred metric scaling on the field that enabled observers to judge the size of other nonbiological objects appearing elsewhere in the context of the ground texture. Results were replicated using actual trees outdoors, pictures of actual trees, and computer generated simulations. In all cases, judgments were accurate at near distances and increasingly underestimated tree size at greater distances. The authors hypothesize that it becomes increasingly difficult to resolve differences in the size and distance of trees as the density of ground texture elements and of branches becomes high. The results of a single study support this surmise. The authors suggest that the accelerating compression of the previous judgment curves was due largely to this effect.

The scaling problem in visual space perception derives from the fact that spatial metrics are absent in optical patterns. Spatial extents in the optic array are angular, not

Correspondence should be addressed to Geoffrey P. Bingham, Department of Psychology, Indiana University, 1101 East 10th Street, Bloomington, IN 47405–7007. E-mail: gbingham@indiana.edu

linear. This is why image size by itself cannot provide information about the corresponding object size. A proposed solution to this problem was formulated by Kepler (following his analysis of image formation by lenses; as cited in Lombardo, 1987). The solution was to impose a linear spatial metric on the optics using the viewing geometry and the positions and orientations of the eyes as they fixate on a common locus in the surrounds. This is binocular vergence, and the resulting metric unit is the distance between the two eyes. This is the unit traditionally implicit in size–distance invariance theory, which uses the distance metric, image size, and viewing geometry to derive object size and, potentially, a metric scaling for the spatial surrounds (Hochberg, 1961; Palmer, 1999). A general scaling could be obtained, for instance, from determination of the size of ground surface texture elements.

Most solutions to the scaling problem in space perception are similar in imposing a metric on the optics using viewing geometry and a dimension of the observer's body or its movement. For instance, the horizon ratio entails the eye height of the observer (Schiff, 1980). Similarly, absolute scale could be obtained from motion parallax using the amplitude (or speed) of observer movement.

The notable alternative to these solutions is familiar size theory, which holds that the size of a recognizable object is simply known (Hochberg, 1961; Palmer, 1999; Schiff, 1980). This solution entails the assumption that given types of objects are invariably of a given size. In turn, this entails constraints that yield the invariance (Bingham, 1993b). Familiar objects are often human artifacts whose size is functionally constrained by human uses and thus by human scale. Implicitly, physical and functional constraints on human scale thus constrain the scale of such familiar objects. By direct extension, other nonhuman biological objects might be constrained in size in a similar way. The problem is that biological objects are subject to growth and thus large changes in size. Thus, mere recognition of a familiar animal or plant would determine its size only within a potentially large range allowed by normal growth from the infant to the adult form or from the seedling to the towering oak.

In the 1970s and early 1980s, Robert E. Shaw and his colleagues attacked this problem and showed that familiar size as applied to biological objects is not limited to specifying only the range of possible sizes entailed by growth. Instead, the particular scale within the range allowed by growth can be perceived. The solution was allometric and was inspired by the work of D'Arcy Thompson (1917/1961) described in his book *On Growth and Form*. Properties of the forms of objects are preserved in optical images and provide information allowing familiar objects to be recognized. Thus, form is the basis of the familiar size solution to the scaling problem. *Allometry* is the study of the way biological forms necessarily change or transform to preserve function in the face of physical changes that occur with changes in size (Niklas, 1994). Because form changes covary with scale changes, forms can be used as information about scale.

Galileo (1638/1914) provided an early example of allometry. He observed that although the weight of a bone is proportional to its volume and thus to the cube of its linear dimension, the strength of the bone or its ability to support the weight is proportional to its cross sectional area and thus to the square of its linear dimension. As the size of a bone is increased, its weight increases much more rapidly than its strength if its shape is unaltered, that is, if the relation between volume and cross-sectional area stays the same. The result is that the bone would fail. To preserve its function, the strength of the bone must be increased in proportion to its weight, and this, in turn, means that the shape must be transformed as the size is increased to keep the cross-sectional area in proportion to the volume.

Shaw's studies focused more on event perception than on space perception. (Shaw, McIntyre, & Mace, 1974). He was interested in the perception of growth as a slow event, describing it in the same way that any event would be characterized, that is, in terms of a continuous transformation. He and his coinvestigators investigated the ability of observers to detect this transformation and use it to judge the age level of various animals, including humans. They investigated perception of age level either from changes in the entire body (Pittenger & Todd, 1983) or from changes in only the head (Mark, Todd, & Shaw, 1981; Pittenger & Shaw, 1975a, 1975b; Pittenger, Shaw, & Mark, 1979; Pittenger & Todd, 1983; Shaw, Mark, Jenkins, & Mingolla, 1982; Shaw & Pittenger, 1977, 1978). Growth of the head was modeled as a cardioidal strain transformation that was chosen to capture the effects of the forces acting on the head during growth (Shaw et al., 1982). Allometry is essentially the study of dynamic similitude that defines similarity in terms of the underlying dynamics rather than the geometry of an object or the kinematics of an event. The geometry or kinematics transform with changes in size as the dynamical configuration of forces is kept invariant. Shaw et al. found that observers were able to judge age level from head or body shape. However, they did not investigate whether observers could judge body size.

Bingham (1993a, 1993b) investigated whether the allometric form solution to the scaling problem would generalize to the traditional space perception problems of size and distance perception. He also investigated whether the solution would generalize to plants and in particular to trees. The value of testing tree perception, in particular, is that trees span a large range of sizes from 1 m to over 30 m in height. Thus, a large range of sizes and distances could be tested. Furthermore, Bingham investigated whether the perceived tree sizes would confer an absolute scaling on the elements of a ground texture gradient in which the tree appeared so that the size of other nonbiological objects appearing elsewhere on the ground at other distances might be judged. Two different allometric relations were relevant to tree forms. One was an elastic similarity scaling that determined the thickness of tree trunks and branches as a function of the tree size. The other was a surface law that determined the numerocity of terminal branches also as a function of tree size. These relations and the resulting tree forms were found to enable observers to judge both tree sizes and the sizes of other nonbiological objects appearing at other distances along a common ground texture.

Although observers did judge tree sizes reliably and fairly accurately, the judgments tended to increasingly underestimate tree sizes as the trees became increasingly distant. That is, for larger trees viewed at greater distance, the judgments became increasingly compressed relative to the actual range of tree sizes. We now hypothesize that this result was a function of the increasing density of the optical ground texture. The idea is that the density of the optical ground texture made it difficult to resolve differences in distance. Image size was controlled in Bingham (1993a, 1993b) by holding it constant. Thus, larger trees were viewed at larger distance and the branching of the trees was also dense. Thus, there may have been similar difficulty in resolving differences in size.

We now investigate this hypothesis. This test also provides additional evidence that tree form as information about tree size scales the entire field, including all objects appearing in the context of the same ground texture. The paradigm was to present observers with displays consisting of three simulated trees appearing in the context of a simulated ground texture (see Figure 1). The simulations were generated as described in Bingham (1993a, 1993b). Two of the trees appeared on the left and right sides of the display. These trees were always placed correctly within the ground texture gradient given the trees actual (modeled) size and their image size. The third tree was placed in the middle of the display and at one of seven distances along the ground texture. Assuming the scaling established by the two trees to the left and right, three of the distances of the middle tree were too close to the viewer given the actual size and image size of the tree, three of the distances were too far, and one of the distances was correct. Observers were asked to judge whether the middle tree appeared at the correct distance given the sizes and distance of the left and right trees. Observers were also asked to rate their confidence in judging the correctness of the placement. Three different correct locations were tested: near, medium, and far. The expectation was that observers would be better able to judge the near set of locations than the far set of locations.

METHOD

Participants

Sixteen undergraduates at Indiana University participated in the experiment. Eight were men and 8 were women. All had normal or corrected to normal vision. Participants were paid at $5 per hr.

Display Generation

The methods for generating the trees and ground texture are described in detail in Bingham (1993a, 1993b). Two different models governing trunk/branch thickness and numerocity, respectively, were used to "grow" simulated trees of heights from

FIGURE 1   Examples of the displays. Trees on the left and right are correctly located along the ground texture gradient given their modeled actual size and image size. The target tree to be judged is in the middle. The target tree is of medium size (top). The target tree is correctly located (bottom). The target tree is located incorrectly along the ground texture gradient. It is in a position that is too near.

7.72 m to 30.48 m. Three of the seven architectures from Bingham (1993b) were used: V, C, and P. The first two simulate deciduous trees like maples or oaks and the last simulates a pine. Trees appeared on a simulated ground texture that was a flat plane covered by tufts of grass.

Each display consisted of three trees. A target tree appeared in the middle of the display. Three different correct target distances were simulated for each of the three architectures. Because the image sizes were held constant, viewing distances were determined by simulated tree heights: a 7.72 m tree at near distance (≈7.01 m), a 16.76 m tree at medium distance (≈14.63 m), and a 27.43 m tree at far distance (≈23.46 m). Target trees (of the same actual heights and image sizes) were also presented at six different incorrect distances (locations on the ground texture), three too close and three too far. The near distances were 3.02 m, 3.69 m, 4.82 m, 6.98 m (correct), 10.21 m 13.47 m, and 16.70 m. The medium distances were 6.19 m, 7.72 m, 10.0 m, 14.75 m (correct), 21.92 m, 29.05 m, and 36.18 m. The far distances were 9.72 m, 11.95 m, 15.85 m, 23.41 m (correct), 34.87 m, 46.33 m, and 57.79 ft. Two other trees appeared to either side of the target tree. These were of the other two architectures, respectively. Each of these trees were of heights different from any of the target heights, one selected from a range between small and medium and the other from a range between medium and large. Each of the remaining two architectures for each target appeared both to the left and the right and at heights from both ranges. This yielded four "frames" for each target architecture. These frames were randomly assigned to the set of target and test distances for each target architecture. Three architectures times three target distances times seven test distances would yield 63 displays. Displays were printed as high contrast black and white images on 8.5 in. × 11 in. paper. However, the greatest test distance at the far target distance was not included because the trees appeared to sit right on the horizon and the display was simply exceptional.

Procedure

Each participant sat before a table on which a stack of the images was placed. Displays were organized in random orders. The judgment task was described to the participant, who was told that the trees to the left and right were placed correctly and the task was to judge the middle tree relative to the other two and decide whether it appeared at the correct distance along the ground given its size. The participant judged the correctness of each display (yes or no) and then flipped it over and to the side to view the next display. After going through the entire set, the participant went back through and adjusted his or her judgments and also judged on a scale of 1 (*not so wrong*) to 5 (*very wrong*) how wrongly placed each tree was if it was judged incorrect, or if it was judged to be correctly placed, the participant judged his or her confidence of this on a scale of 1 (*not confident*) to 5 (*confident*).

RESULTS AND DISCUSSION

We performed analysis first on the adjusted correctness judgments and second on the wrongness and confidence judgments. The mean proportions of displays judged as correct is shown in Figure 2. (*Note:* To judge as correct here is not necessarily to judge correctly.) The result was that correctly and incorrectly placed trees were distinguished at the near and medium distances but not at the far distance. At the near distance, the location that was just closer than the correct location was judged as correct most often, that is, 85% of the time. The location that was actually correct was judged correct only 58% of the time. Locations that were increasingly too close or too distant were increasingly judged as incorrect. The most distant location was judged as incorrect 71% of the time. At the medium distance, the correct location was judged as correct 75% of the time. Locations closer and farther than this were judged as correct increasingly less often as the misplacement increased. Finally, at the large distance, all locations were judged essentially at chance. The correct location was judged as correct 54% of the time. The most incorrect location was also judged as incorrect 54% of the time.

We performed a mixed design analysis of variance (ANOVA) on these judgments with gender as a between-subjects factor and test distance (7 levels), target distance (3 levels), and architecture (3 levels) as repeated measures factors. Test distance was significant, $F(6, 84) = 4.4, p < .001$. Overall, correct distances were judged as correct more often than incorrect distances. Architecture was signifi-

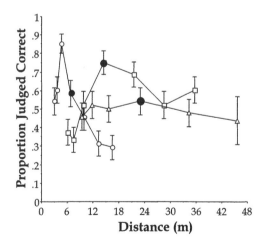

FIGURE 2   Mean proportions of judgments that the target tree is in the correct location plotted as a function of simulated viewing distance. A 0.5 proportion is chance. Means were averaged across the three architectures. The near set of locations is plotted as open circles, the medium set as open squares, and the far set as open triangles. A large back dot in each case marks the correct location in each set. Error bars are standard errors.

cant, $F(2, 28) = 3.8, p < .05$. Architecture P (pine) was judged as correct more often than the other two architectures. The test distance by target distance interaction was significant, $F(12, 168) = 3.5, p < .001$. As shown in Figure 2, correct test distances were distinguished at the near and medium target distances but not at the far target distance. Finally, the test distance by architecture interaction was significant, $F(12, 168) = 2.0, p < .05$. Incorrect near test distances were judged as correct more often for the P architecture than for either the C or V architecture.

The pattern of results was essentially the same once the wrongness and confidence judgments were taken into account. Recall that if a display was judged as incorrect then a wrongness judgment was required between 1 (*less wrong*) and 5 (*most wrong*), and if a display was judged correct then a confidence judgment was required between 1 (*maybe correct*) and 5 (*certainly correct*). We multiplied wrongness judgments by −1, and then, for each of the 20 tree locations, we combined these negative wrongness judgments with the confidence judgments; that is, if the display was judged incorrect then there was a corresponding negative wrongness value, and if the display was judged correct then there was a corresponding positive confidence value. Means were computed for each of the 20 possible tree locations, and these were plotted in Figure 3. The wrongness and confidence judgments simply replicated the proportions of correctness judgments. Using two-tailed t tests, we tested the means at each of the 20 locations for difference from 0. Counting from left to right the 7 means in Figure 3 for each of the three target distances (near,

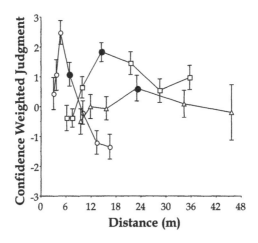

FIGURE 3   Mean judgments are weighted by negative mean wrongness judgments if the location is judged incorrect and by positive confidence judgments if the location is judged correct. A mean of 0 indicates inability to judge correctness of the location on average. Means were averaged across the three architectures. The near set of locations is plotted as open circles, the medium set as open squares, and the far set as open triangles. A large back dot in each case marks the correct location in each set. Error bars are standard errors.

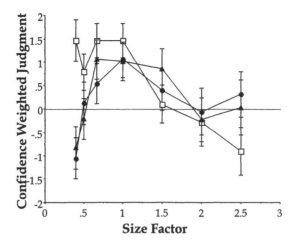

FIGURE 4   Mean judgments are weighted by negative mean wrongness judgments if the location is judged incorrect and by positive confidence judgments if the location is judged correct. A mean of 0 indicates inability to judge correctness of the location on average. Means were averaged across the three viewing distances. The means for architecture P are plotted as open squares, for architecture C as filled circles, and for architecture V as filled triangles. Means are plotted as a function of the size factor, that is, the actual size specified by the location along the texture gradient together with the image size (but not the form of the tree). A size factor of 1 means that the size specified by the form of the tree is the same as that specified by the location along the ground texture gradient together with the image size. Error bars are standard errors.

medium, and far): the 3rd, 6th, and 7th means were different from 0 ($p < .05$) at the near distance; the 1st, 2nd, 4th, and 5th means were different from 0 ($p < .05$) at the medium distance; and only the 1st mean was different from 0 ($p < .05$) at the far distance. When we performed the same mixed design ANOVA on these data as before, the pattern of results was the same as for the correctness judgments. Significant main effects were obtained for test distance, $F(6, 78) = 6.1, p < .001$; and architecture, $F(2, 26) = 4.3, p < .05$. Significant interactions were found for test distance by target distance, $F(12, 156) = 4.1, p < .001$; and test distance by architecture, $F(12, 156) = 3.8, p < .001$. Means for each of the architectures by test distance are shown in Figure 4.

GENERAL DISCUSSION

There were two goals for this study. First, we intended to confirm the results of the previous studies showing both that allometric tree forms provide information about tree size and that this scaling information confers a metric scale on elements in a ground texture gradient. The latter yields a metric scaling of the entire field. The results of this study confirmed this finding. The two correctly placed trees on the left and right sides of the displays scaled the entire field so as to enable observers to judge whether the target tree placed in the middle of the display was in fact correctly located along the ground plane given both the form (and thus perceptible size) and the image size of the tree.

Second, we tested the hypothesis that trees at increasing distances along the ground plane become more difficult to discriminate in terms of their size and distance. This would be expected simply from Weber scaling of the corresponding ground texture density, tree branching density, and relative increment size of trunk and branch thickness. For instance, Weber ratios for changes in terminal branch numbers over successive generations are near 1 for the smallest trees but below 20% for the largest trees. The results were that indeed distant trees were discriminated only at chance whereas trees at near or medium distances were successfully discriminated as being placed correctly or incorrectly within the field.

Two results obtained in this study were not anticipated. The first is shown in Figure 4. Incorrectly near locations were tolerated for the pine tree architecture and judged as correct. This did not occur with the other two (deciduous) architectures. A comparison of the displays for the small target trees for each of the three architectures is shown in Figure 5 in which the target trees appear in the nearest incorrect location. In Figure 5, it is evident that the thickness of the pine tree trunk appears rather less than that of the other two tree types. This is due directly to the architectural differences in branch geometry. The branching angles are much larger in the pine so the initial branches depart more rapidly from the trunk, making the trunk appear relatively thinner than in the other two architectures in which, because of the shallow branching angles, the initial branches essentially combine with the trunk to increase its effective thickness. The results show clearly that observers are using this information.

The second unexpected result was that the smallest trees in all three architectures were judged to be correctly located at the position just closer than the modeled correct position. As discussed in Bingham (1993b), the tree growth models used in these simulations are imperfect, and, according to visual assessments reported in that article, the failure is greatest for the smallest trees. Improved models of tree growth and morphology would presumably correct these results.

The bottom line in this study is that the allometric forms of biological objects definitely yield information about spatial scale and thus yield an important solution to the scaling problem in space perception. Physical constraints on natural geometry generate structure that remains invariant in optical patterns and enables perceivers to remain grounded in the natural world. Gibson (1973) argued that formless invariants provide detectable information for perceivers. These are the continuous transformations studied by Shaw in the context of growth as a slow event. Shaw pursued Gibson's insight in search of what Runeson (1977/1983) sub-

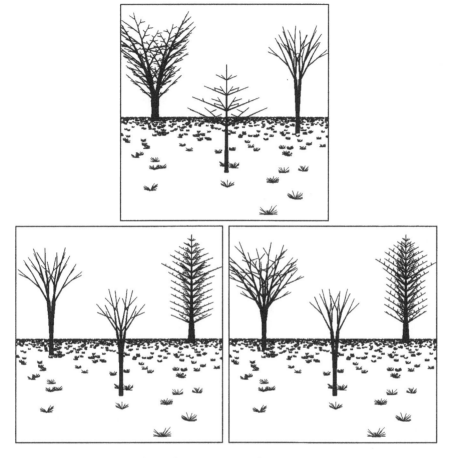

FIGURE 5   Examples of the small target trees in each of the three architectures all located along the ground texture gradient at an incorrect near location. The top panel is architecture P. The bottom left panel is architecture C. The bottom right panel is architecture V.

sequently called "informational bases" (Runeson & Frykholm, 1983). Shaw found his basis in allometry. He (and Runeson, too) showed that the abstract is ultimately very concrete, and this is the basis for meaning in information. What a marvelous idea this was, intuited by Gibson and fleshed out by Shaw and Runeson.

ACKNOWLEDGMENT

This work was supported by Grant R01 EY11741–01A3 from the National Eye Institute.

REFERENCES

Bingham, G. P. (1993a). Perceiving the size of trees: Biological form and the horizon ratio. *Perception & Psychophysics, 54,* 485–495.

Bingham, G. P. (1993b). Perceiving the size of trees: Form as information about scale. *Journal of Experimental Psychology: Human Perception and Performance, 19,* 1139–1161.

Galileo, G. (1914). *Dialogues concerning two new sciences.* New York: Dover. (Original work published 1638)

Gibson, J. J. (1973). On the concept of "formless invariants" in visual perception. *Leonardo, 6,* 43–45.

Hochberg, J. (1961). *Perception.* Englewood Cliffs, NJ: Prentice Hall.

Lombardo, T. J. (1987). *The reciprocity of perceiver and environment: The evolution of James J. Gibson's ecological psychology.* Hillsdale, NJ: Lawrence Erlbaum Associates, Inc.

Mark, L. S., Todd, J. T., & Shaw, R. E. (1981). Perception of growth: A geometric analysis of how different styles of change are distinguished. *Journal of Experimental Psychology: Human Perception and Performance, 7,* 855–868.

Niklas, K. J. (1994). *Plant allometry: The scaling of form and process.* Chicago: University of Chicago Press.

Palmer, S. E. (1999). *Vision science: Photons to phenomonology.* Cambridge, MA: MIT Press.

Pittenger, J. B., & Shaw, R. E. (1975a). Aging faces as viscal-elastic events: Implication for a theory of nonrigid shape perception. *Journal of Experimental Psychology: Human Perception and Performance, 1,* 374–382.

Pittenger, J. B., & Shaw, R. E. (1975b). Perception of relative and absolute age in facial photographs. *Perception & Psychophysics, 18,* 137–143.

Pittenger, J. B., Shaw, R. E., & Mark, L. S. (1979). Perceptual information for the age level of faces as a higher order invariant of growth. *Journal of Experimental Psychology: Human Perception and Performance, 5,* 478–493.

Pittenger, J. B., & Todd, J. T. (1983). Perception of growth from changes in body proportions. *Journal of Experimental Psychology: Human Perception and Performance, 9,* 945–954.

Runeson, S. (1977/1983). *On the visual perception of dynamic events* (Acta Universitatis Upsaliensis: Studia Psycholgica Upsaliensia, Serial No. 9).

Runeson, S., & Frykholm, C. (1983). Kinematic specification of dynamics as an informational basis for person and action perception: Expectation, gender recognition, and deceptive intention. *Journal of Experimental Psychology: General, 112,* 585–615.

Schiff, W. (1980). *Perception: An applied approach.* Boston, MA: Houghton Mifflin.

Shaw, R. E., Mark, L. S., Jenkins, D. H., & Mingolla, E. (1982). A dynamic geometry for predicting growth of gross craniofacial morphology. In A. Dixon & B. Sarnat (Eds.), *Factors and mechanisms influencing bone growth* (pp. 423–431). New York: Academic.

Shaw, R., McIntyre, M., & Mace, W. (1974). The role of symmetry in event perception. In R. MacLeod & H. Pick (Eds.), *Studies in perception: Essays in honor of J. J. Gibson* (pp. 276–310). Ithaca, NY: Cornell University Press.

Shaw, R., & Pittenger, J. (1977). Perceiving the face of change in changing faces: Implications for a theory of object perception. In R. Shaw & J. Bransford (Eds.), *Perceiving, acting, and knowing: Toward an ecological psychology* (pp. 103–132). Hillsdale, NJ: Lawrence Erlbaum Associates, Inc.

Shaw, R., & Pittenger, J. (1978). Perceiving change. In H. L. Pick & E. Saltzman (Eds.), *Modes of perceiving and processing information* (pp. 187–204). Hillsdale, NJ: Lawrence Erlbaum Associates, Inc.

Thompson, D. A. (1961). *On growth and form.* Cambridge, England: Cambridge University Press. (Original work published 1917)

ECOLOGICAL PSYCHOLOGY, 17(3 & 4), 205–230

Algorists, Algorithms, and Complexity: An Exploration of the Shavian Critique of Discrete State Computation

A. J. Wells

Department of Social Psychology
The London School of Economics and Political Science

The status of computational theory in ecological psychology has been and continues to be a source of controversy. Over a period of more than 30 years, Robert Shaw and his colleagues have developed a powerful negative critique of computation based in part on the idea that computational theory cannot capture central aspects of the coimplicative structure of the relations between animals and their environments. Two aspects of the Shavian critique are considered in this article: the characterization of the algorist and the problem of complexity. It is argued, contrary to the critique, that computational theory offers a properly constrained formal view of the algorist and is not defeated by complexity. Computational ideas can therefore have a fundamental role to play in the further development of ecological psychology.

In his final book, *The Ecological Approach to Visual Perception*, J. J. Gibson (1979/1986) introduced the term *mutuality* to describe the linkages between animals and their environments. The concept of mutuality expresses the idea that the linkages are, in some ways, necessary rather than contingent. Gibson suggested, in fact, that *animal* and *environment* are inseparable terms and that each implies the other. One of the central tasks for the ecological approach is, therefore, "to explain how agents are situated, that is, functionally coupled to their environments so as to facilitate adaptive actions" (Shaw, 2003, p. 37). This article is about the kind of formal theory that might be developed to explain the kinds of adaptive functional

---

Correspondence should be addressed to A. J. Wells, Department of Social Psychology, The London School of Economics and Political Science, Houghton Street, London WC2A 2AE, UK. E-mail: a.j.wells@lse.ac.uk

interaction between animals and their environments that are implied by the concept of mutuality.

Mature sciences tend toward the presentation of theories in mathematical form. The many advantages of mathematical presentation include rigor, precision, and clarity. If, as some have said, mathematics is the language of nature, its indispensable role in scientific theories is unsurprising. It is, however, sometimes claimed that certain characteristics of sciences such as psychology and biology make them inappropriate for particular types of mathematical treatment. Penrose (1989, 1994), for example, has argued that aspects of human consciousness are provably uncomputable, and Rosen (1991, 2000) has argued that living systems in general display complexity of a kind that cannot be captured by discrete algorithmic methods. Such arguments point to the need for careful thought about the kind of mathematics that might best be used for the development of psychological theory in general and ecological psychology in particular.

An important strand of theorizing within ecological psychology, to which Robert Shaw has made a major contribution, has examined discrete computational methods as a possible mathematical foundation for psychology. Gibson was opposed to computational accounts of information processing, and Shaw and various colleagues in articles published over a period of more than 30 years have given reasons for thinking that Gibson's opposition was well founded. The more recent work of theorists such as Penrose and Rosen is used to support the arguments Shaw and his colleagues have developed. Shaw has been the principal architect of an account of the functional coupling of agents and their environments in terms of duality and coalitions that, he argues, provides the mathematical foundation on which ecological psychology should be built. His approach, as he has said recently, (Shaw, 2003, p. 102) does not entirely rule out a role for a computational form of ecological psychology but suggests that it will be peripheral. Those who, like me, believe that computational mathematics can have a central part to play in the development of ecological psychology need to examine the anticomputational tradition and to tackle the problems it raises.

I am going to call the body of work by Shaw and his colleagues that has examined computational methods "the Shavian critique of computation." In doing this, I am in no sense wishing to minimize the important contributions of Shaw's coauthors. Some of the articles in which the critique has been center stage include as coauthors Claudia Carello, Peter Kugler, Michael McIntyre, Michael Turvey, and James Todd. However, the major themes with which this article is concerned are recurrent aspects of Shaw's oeuvre from 1969 onward, and his contributions to the critique of computation and to the alternative approach via coalitions have been pivotal.

The major foci of this article are two aspects of the Shavian critique: the characterization of the algorist or knower and the problem of complexity. In outline, the Shavian critique presents the following argument: The formal theory of computation developed by Turing (1936) and others in the 1930s fails to specify the role of the agent or knower because abstract automata do not satisfy the natural constraints that must be satisfied by real agents. At the very least, therefore, computational methods must be supplemented by an account of these constraints. However, even if such an account can be given, the standard computational approach to psychological functioning remains vulnerable because it assumes that simple and complex systems are equally amenable to explanation by computational modeling. Von Neumann's (1966) conjecture strongly suggested that computational methods are viable only for systems of low complexity. Because the situated human agent is a highly complex system it is suggested that computational methods cannot provide the right type of explanation. Instead, it is argued, the appropriate theoretical foundation for ecological psychology is a formalized account of coalitions.

The response made to the Shavian critique, again in outline, is the following: The importance of the algorist and the challenge of Von Neumann's (1966) conjecture are accepted. However, it is argued, contrary to the critique, that Turing's analysis of computation in his famous article of 1936 does in fact provide a rigorous account of the algorist. Once this is understood, the ground is cleared for a computational account of ecological psychology that is properly constrained. It is also argued that Von Neumann's conjecture can be understood in a way that is consistent with the use of computational methods. Such an interpretation of the conjecture is more consistent with other aspects of Von Neumann's thinking than the interpretations that Shaw discusses. The new approach to the conjecture rests on a distinction between structural and behavioral descriptions of complex systems. Structural descriptions are finite, but behavioral descriptions may be infinite. The existence of undecidable predicates shows that explanations of the behavior of complex systems cannot be given in full a priori, but this does not imply that complex systems must exhibit uncomputable behavior. Seen from this fresh perspective, the limits of formal inquiry provide the basis for an integration of the "what," "how," and "who" questions that Shaw and McIntyre (1974) posed for psychologists. The agent or "epistemic who" is modeled by the finite control of the Turing machine. What is known and how it is known are facets of the situated agent and the relation of mutuality between the agent and the environment. Von Neumann's insights also suggest that the study of the functional architecture of the brain should be part of the research agenda of ecological psychology.

CHARACTERIZING THE ALGORIST

What is known and *how* it is known are relative questions that make no sense independent of the question of *who* knows. Indeed, our opinion is that the central question of cognitive psychology concerns the essential nature of a knowing-agent, rather than just what is known or even how what is known *is* known. (Shaw & McIntyre, 1974, p. 305)

Quite so! Thirty years on we should applaud the clarity of vision that this open-ing sentence of "Algoristic Foundations to Cognitive Psychology" demonstrates. Psychological research methods, the demands of career development, and the nar-row targeting of research funds all tend to lead to a focus on details, a focus that can be to the detriment of theoretical concern for the whole person, the ultimate sub-ject of psychological theory. It was a characteristically bold move for Shaw and McIntyre to locate the whole person at the center of their article. They suggested that there was no consensus about the interrelationship of the what, how, and who questions or about how to tackle them and thus no clear picture of the whole per-son. They described how existing approaches to the what question were couched broadly in terms of information and those to the how question broadly in terms of algorithms but suggested that the neglected who question could serve as a theoreti-cal fulcrum to provide an integrated attack on all three.

> If we can even roughly decide on the nature of the epistemic-who we will, at the same time, *have* to take a stand on the nature of the information processed from and about the environment, as well as on the nature of the psychological processes required to do so. (Shaw & McIntyre, 1974, pp. 307–308)

Shaw and McIntyre characterized Gibson's ecological optics as an attempt to study the what of perception and contrasted his approach with those of a number of constructivist theorists, including Sperling, Neisser, and Broadbent, who they characterized as concerned with the how question. They argued that the union of these two types of approaches left the who question untouched. To tackle the who question, they proposed to relate the class of knowing systems to various classes of automata, making en route a crucial distinction between what they called *algorith-mic* and *algoristic* approaches to psychological processes. The two terms distin-guished a large set of processes (the *algorithms*) that is characterized solely by the satisfaction of mechanistic relations between input and output from a subset (the *algorisms*) whose members are those algorithms that also satisfy the constraints un-der which human agents function, for example, the constraints of evolution and natural law. The class of algorithms, according to Shaw and McIntyre, is "obviously much larger than the class of machines that may be physically realized by construc-tion as artifacts or by natural evolution" (p. 310), and, in consequence, "the algo-rithmic bases of cognitive processes can only be defined relative to what we wish to call their *algoristic* bases" (p. 315). Another way to make this point is to say that the algorithmic level of analysis cannot be fundamental for psychology because it pre-supposes the algoristic level. Shaw and McIntyre confirmed this interpretation as their intended meaning a little further on in the article when they said that "the in-tuitive notion of algorithm rests ultimately on what is meant by an epistemic agent, or algorist" (p. 316). It follows, if this line of argument is correct, that it is essential to characterize the algoristic bases of cognitive processes that is the set of constraints that picks out the algorisms from the larger set of algorithms. Moreover, as Shaw and McIntyre also noted, there are constraints arising from the properties of energy distributions in the environment that further limit the set of humanly realizable algorithms. The ultimate target sought is the specification of a system that computes "natural" algorithms, that is those "functions satisfying both the natural cost parameters and intentionality of physically, biologically, and psychologically realizable systems" (p. 320). Shaw and McIntyre argued that the development of an adequate theory of the algorist had to go beyond the theory of computation and might transcend the then-current understanding of physical and biological laws.

An immediate consequence of this argument is that algorithmic, that is, computational, specifications of processes do not satisfy the constraints under which natural agents function. Computational processes are therefore, at best, incomplete as a foundation for psychology. Shaw and McIntyre (1974) were quite explicit about this with respect to Turing machines. They discussed the Church–Turing thesis and acknowledged the fundamental logical result that every scheme proposed as a formal model of the intuitive notion of an effective procedure turns out to compute exactly those functions computable by a universal Turing machine. They then posed the question, "Does this mean then that the universal Turing machine and the class of abstract automata equivalent to it provide a rigorous instantiation of what we intuitively mean by an algorist?" (Shaw & McIntyre, 1974, p. 317). The rhetorical tone of the question suggests the negative answer that swiftly followed. Turing machines, they said, do not capture the properties of algorists because

> such abstract automata do not satisfy the natural constraints that must be satisfied by any real agent. For instance, Turing machines are assumed to possess infinite memory capacity, to be perfectly reliable, and to compute as fast as you please—all ideal properties not representative of any organism or actual machine. (p. 317)

The algorist article (Shaw & McIntyre, 1974) has been influential in ecological psychology, and its arguments have contributed to the rejection of computational theory as a suitable mathematical basis for the ecological approach. I agree completely with Shaw and McIntyre about the need for a formal theory that respects the constraints under which agents operate, and their article is an early and important statement of the naturalistic constraints that any psychological theory needs to respect. I part company with them, however, with respect to the status of the Turing machine. Our difference in this respect is fundamental. I shall demonstrate that Turing's (1936) theory does in fact contain a model of the algorist that satisfies natural constraints. The algorisms are coextensive with the algorithms, as these were defined by Turing, not a proper subset of them, as Shaw and McIntyre suggest.

Turing's theory thus provides, in principle at least, a suitable mathematical foundation for ecological psychology.

The difference of approach stems largely, I believe, from the fact that contemporary scholars have greater access than did our colleagues in the 1970s to Turing's (1936) own article. It may also be relevant that Shaw and McIntyre are members of the American rather than the British academic community. It is noteworthy, for example, that they cite directly the articles of Church (1936) and Kleene (1936), which were published in American journals, but do not cite Turing's equally fundamental article (Turing, 1936), which was published in the *Proceedings of the London Mathematical Society*, a journal that was, presumably, much less accessible to American scholars. My supposition is that when Shaw and McIntyre wrote their article they knew of Turing's work from sources other than his own writings. Had they had the chance to study and think about his article directly, they might, I surmise, have come to different views about the relation between algorithms and algorists and ecological psychology might have taken a different, more computational turn. Turing's work is unique among the founding documents of computer science for the way in which it relates the function computed to the agent doing the computing. For this reason, the distinction between algorithm and algorist does not apply to Turing in the way that it appears to apply to the systems of Church and Kleene, despite the formal equivalences between their approaches and that of Turing.

TURING'S ANALYSIS OF COMPUTATION AND THE MODELING OF THE ALGORIST

Shaw and McIntyre (1974) were critical of the Turing machine as a basis for the formal specification of the algorist because the machine model was said not to satisfy the natural constraints that must be satisfied by any natural agent. The Turing machine's infinite memory and perfect reliability were cited as instances of this failure. A different understanding can be derived from Turing's (1936) fundamental article "On Computable Numbers With an Application to the Entscheidungsproblem." The article is now available in the volume of Turing's collected works containing his articles in mathematical logic (Gandy & Yates, 2001). Turing's analysis of the process of routine computation was an ecological analysis that gave equal weight to the environment and to the algorist. Moreover, the design of the Turing machine specifically reflects natural constraints arising from both the agent and the environment. It will become apparent, strange as it may sound, that the infinite memory and the perfect reliability of the machine are quite consistent with the satisfaction of natural constraints. A short account of Turing's analysis is given here. A more detailed exposition can be found in Wells (2004). The best starting point is Turing's own description of a machine whose purpose was to compute exactly those real numbers that could be computed "effectively" by a human working with paper and pencil. He said,

> We may compare a man in the process of computing a real number to a machine which is only capable of a finite number of conditions q_1, q_2, ... , q_R which will be called "m-configurations." The machine is supplied with a "tape" (the analogue of paper) running through it, and divided into sections (called "squares") each capable of bearing a "symbol." At any moment there is just one square, say the r-th, bearing the symbol $S(r)$ which is "in the machine." We may call this square the "scanned" square. The symbol on the scanned square may be called the "scanned symbol." The "scanned symbol" is the only one of which the machine is, so to speak, "directly aware." However, by altering its m-configuration the machine can effectively remember some of the symbols which it has "seen" (scanned) previously. The possible behavior of the machine at any moment is determined by the m-configuration q_n and the scanned symbol $S(r)$. This pair q_n, $S(r)$ will be called the "configuration": thus the configuration determines the possible behavior of the machine. In some of the configurations in which the scanned square is blank (*i.e.* bears no symbol) the machine writes down a new symbol on the scanned square: in other configurations it erases the scanned symbol. The machine may also change the square which is being scanned, but only by shifting it one place to right or left. In addition to any of these operations the m-configuration may be changed. (Turing, 1936, p. 231)

This excerpt provides the key to understanding the ecological basis of Turing's analysis of paper and pencil calculations. A person carrying out a calculation is compared to a machine with a finite number of "conditions," as Turing calls them. In modern terminology they are called functional states. Each is given a unique name. The finite state machine is Turing's model of the mind of the algorist. The paper on which the workings and results of the calculation are written down is replaced by a one-dimensional tape divided into squares. The tape is Turing's model of the environment. Each square of the tape is either blank or contains a symbol from a finite alphabet that the machine is able to recognize. It cannot be emphasized too strongly that the tape is distinct from the finite machine, although the two are connected. A person doing a calculation is distinct from the paper on which the calculation is worked, although they are connected via the processes of reading and writing. So it is with the finite machine and its tape. The machine is "directly aware" of one square of the tape at a time and can read what is on that square and write something on it. It can move the tape, one square at a time, so as to change the square of which it is directly aware. The machine can also change its functional state. The behavior of the machine is determined by its current functional state and the contents of the square of the tape of which it is currently aware. This pair is called a "configuration." It relates both to the algorist and to the environment and provides a striking formal model of a Gibsonian affordance. See Wells (2002) for a detailed exposition of this idea.

Turing machines have a single perceptual capacity: the capacity to read or recognize symbols from a fixed finite alphabet. This capacity is a model of the perceptual processes of a human algorist carrying out a paper and pencil calculation. The capacity is defined in a purely functional fashion. Nothing is said about how symbol recognition might be instantiated in a real physical machine. Turing machines have two action capacities: the capacity to write or print symbols from the alphabet and the capacity to move the machine relative to the tape. These capacities are models of the activity of the algorist. Nothing is said about how these capacities might be physically instantiated. Reading, writing, and moving are capacities that connect the machine to the tape. Turing machines are also able to change from one functional state to another, modeling changes of state of mind of the algorist in a way that is described by rules. Turing says nothing about the physical realization of the functional states or of the means by which changes of state are achieved.

The differences between physical and functional descriptions of a system and the nature of the abstraction involved in a functional description are clearly illustrated by the everyday light switch. A light switch is a physical system with many parts. Many physically different kinds of switches can be made that are designed to have two distinct functional states, on and off. Turing described the nature of the abstraction involved in moving from physical to functional description.

> Everything really moves continuously. But there are many kinds of machine which can profitably be *thought of* as being discrete state machines. For instance in considering the switches for a lighting system it is a convenient fiction that each switch must be definitely on or definitely off. There must be intermediate positions, but for most purposes we can forget about them. (Turing, 1950, p. 439)

A functional description can be used as the basis for a physical realization, or a functional description can be abstracted from an existing physical system. The latter was the route that Turing took in the analysis of computation that he carried out for the 1936 article. The physical system was the human algorist performing a calculation, and the functional description that Turing abstracted was a machine with a finite number of functional states. The output of a Turing machine is of two kinds. There is the sequence of zeroes and ones that constitutes the binary representation of the real number computed by the machine. Once a zero or a one has been printed it is not erased and forms a permanent part of the sequence. Turing machines also print a variety of other symbols for various purposes, much as one might write down a carry digit when doing a large addition. These temporary symbols are eventually erased. Turing made an important distinction between machines that keep printing zeroes and ones ad infinitum, which he called "circle-free" machines, and those that print only a finite number of zeroes and ones, which he called "circular" machines. The potentially infinite sequence of digits output by a circle-free machine is produced by the interaction between the finite state control and the tape. Because the finite state control has a fixed number of functional states, the machine has to cycle through its functional states many times in order to produce its potentially infinite output.

The determination of behavior by configurations (ordered pairs of functional states and tape symbols) is straightforward to state but easy to misinterpret. Each possible configuration of a Turing machine has a set of actions associated with it. The combination of a configuration and its associated actions is called an "instruction" and the complete set of instructions defining the behavior of a machine is called a "machine table." A starting configuration is specified for each Turing machine and the actions associated with it lead to the next configuration with its associated actions and so on. It is customary to describe Turing machines as "rule governed" because each instruction can be called a rule of behavior. However, it is misleading to think of a Turing machine's behavior as being governed by explicit rules except in the special case of universal machines. The concept of a rule of behavior should be understood in the sense that Gibson intended when he talked about rules for the control of behavior. In "The Ecological Approach to Visual Perception" (Gibson, 1979/1986), he described the problem of expressing the appropriate sense of the term "rule" with respect to the visual control of locomotion:

> I asserted that behavior was controlled by *rules*. Surely, however, they are not rules enforced by an authority. The rules are not commands from a brain; they emerge from the animal–environment system. But the only way to describe rules is in words, and a rule expressed in words is a command. I am faced with a paradox. The rules for the control of locomotion will sound like commands, although they are not intended to. I can only suggest that the reader should interpret them as rules *not formulated in words*. (pp. 232–233)

The rules for control of the behavior of a Turing machine express the actions needed to produce a specific outcome. They are not rules formulated in symbols, to adapt Gibson's phrase, but are emergent properties of the combined system of the machine and its tape. This characteristic makes the Turing machine a suitable mathematical foundation for ecological psychology. Looking out of my window, I can see a swift, *Apus apus*, hawking insects in the air above the building on the other side of the road. Its behavior is controlled by an interaction between the states of its brain and the states of its environment. One fundamental contention of this article is that Turing machines provide a suitable foundation for the study of such interactions. The brain of the swift can be described in terms of a set of functional states, the states of its environment can be described in terms of locations and their contents, and the behavior of the swift can be described as a sequence of configurations and associated actions. There is much to be added to this basic account including the important fact that the swift's behavior is nondeterministic, but that does not undermine the fundamental appropriateness of computational description. Please notice also that the characterization of the neural states of the swift as the functional states of a biological machine does not imply that those states consist of internal symbolic rules or that the swift has an internal symbolic representation of its environment.

The characterization of functional states and the distinction between universal Turing machines and others are topics that require discussion. The two are related, as will become clear. Cooking provides familiar situations that can be used as examples. Consider, first, the striking fact that I can carry out a sequence of operations that results in a boiled egg without having recourse to explicit instructions. I do this by putting the egg in a pan, adding water, putting the pan on the hob, turning on the gas, and so on. These observable operations are controlled by activity in my central nervous system. The nature of that internal activity is a topic of fundamental debate.

From a standard computational perspective, my brain might be characterized as instantiating an egg boiling production system whose productions break down the task into a sequence of elementary actions such as (PUT (EGG, PAN)) that have explicit symbolic representations somewhere in my memory and are evoked by the state of the environment and my current goal structure. I am not, I repeat NOT, advocating a computational approach of this kind.

From the Gibsonian perspective, my brain might be characterized as resonating to the learned affordances of the egg-boiling situation. The resonance concept is much closer to the kind of computational approach advocated in this article than is the production system model. Resonance, however, implies a rather passive role for the agent, and it is hard to see how to use it to model the exploratory orienting activities that are characteristic of the behavior of organisms. A fundamental suggestion of the computational approach described here is that the concept of resonance can be explored and elaborated within the discrete state framework of the Turing machine formalism. Behavior in the Turing machine model is controlled jointly by the functional states of the finite machine and by the currently perceived part of the environment. Such joint determination seems ideally suited to the task of modeling the situated control of behavior that is characteristic of ecological psychology.

Functional states are discrete because the egg-boiling task consists of a sequence of discrete elementary operations, and the sequence has at least a partial ordering. Putting an egg in the pan is one discrete operation, putting water in the pan is another. It doesn't much matter whether the egg goes in the pan before the water or vice versa, but the water must be in the pan before the heat source is applied, hence the existence of a partial ordering of the operations for a successful outcome. The characterization of functional states as discrete is compatible with a wide range of modes of operation of the underlying physical system in which the abstractly described system might be instantiated. It is, for example, perfectly possible for discrete functional states to be described in systems whose underlying control dynamics are continuous. The different macro states of water resulting from continuous temperature changes are a simple example and the phenomena of categorical perception (Harnad, 1987) provide numerous human examples.

Turing's account of discrete functional states abstracts from the details of physical instantiation but is compatible with any physical realization that preserves the functionality described in a given model. Thus the description of the states of my egg-boiling brain as discrete functional states is compatible with a continuous dynamical description of the underlying neural hardware. It is also compatible with a discrete internal symbolic representation of the task but does not entail one. The activities that I undertake when boiling an egg could be modeled by a nonuniversal Turing machine.

In addition to boiling an egg, I can carry out a sequence of operations that results in a dish of green beans in a spicy tomato sauce called *Masaledar sem* (Jaffrey, 1995). *Masaledar sem* requires a much longer sequence of operations than that needed to boil an egg, and I need to follow instructions to achieve the desired result. In this case, there is an explicit symbolic representation involved in my performance of the task. It is called a recipe. It is located in the environment, and my actions result from reading and carrying out the instructions that constitute the recipe. The capacity to read and execute recipes enormously increases the scope of my cooking without requiring permanent modifications to my mental contents. It is not necessary for me to memorize recipes or to remember them from one occasion of use to another. Provided I have the book available, I have, as it were, a source for many sauces. A universal machine is one whose functional states are organized in such a way that it is able to do something very similar. A universal machine interprets the description of another Turing machine that is written on its tape and behaves as though it were that Turing machine. By changing the description its behavior is changed in essentially the way that changing the recipe with which I work changes what I cook. A universal Turing machine is, nevertheless, just like any other Turing machine with regard to the character of its own functional states. The difference comes in how they are organized and the way the machine uses its tape.

Turing's analysis is striking in its simplicity. It asserts that all that is needed for a mathematical model of a person doing a paper and pencil calculation is a set of functional states modeling the algorist, a tape divided into squares modeling the environment, an alphabet of symbols, and a set of actions determined by the machine's configurations. In what sense can this model be said to satisfy the natural constraints that impinge on a situated agent? Four crucial points of Turing's analysis are relevant here.

First, the set of functional states modeling the mind of the algorist is finite. This, as Turing (1936) said, reflects the fact that "the human memory is necessarily limited" (p. 231). Turing made little in the way of a defense of this contention, but it may be interpreted as a commitment to a physical basis for mental states. Because the brain is a finite organ, if mental states are physical states it follows that there can only be finitely many of them. It is important, in this respect, to note that the requirement for an infinite tape does not contradict this suggestion. The tape is a model of the environment, not of the algorist. Moreover, the tape is not required to be infinite at the start of a computation. It is simply assumed that more squares can be added if required. The specification of an unbounded tape reflects the fact that availability of paper is not part of the definition of an effective calculation. If, for example, we want to write out the decimal expansion of π to an arbitrary degree of precision we will need an infinite supply of paper because π has infinitely many digits.

Second, the number of symbols in the alphabet of a Turing machine has to be finite. This constraint reflects the fact that symbols are to be written on tape squares and squares are of a fixed size. As Turing (1936) said, "If we were to allow an infinity of symbols, then there would be symbols differing to an arbitrarily small extent" (p. 249). This is a straightforward perceptual constraint. The human visual system has a finite resolving capacity. If we had to deal with an infinity of symbols confined to squares of fixed size, the symbols would differ to an arbitrarily small extent. In consequence, effective calculation would cease to be possible because errors of symbol discrimination would occur. It is important to notice the human character of this constraint. It is easy to describe machines that are not subject to human perceptual limitations, and it is possible to imagine machines with infinite resolving capacity for example machines with registers that can store numbers with arbitrary precision. Some theorists have explored the possibility that Turing computability does not exhaust the possibilities of natural computation (cf. Eberbach, Goldin, & Wegner, 2004; Siegelmann, 1999; Stannett, 2004). Super-Turing or hyper-Turing models, as they are sometimes called, result from relaxing one or more of the constraints that Turing identified as necessary for a formal model that could compute all and only those numbers that could be computed by a human algorist working with paper and pencil. It was of the essence of the Turing machine that it respected the constraints on human algorists.

Third, Turing specified a bound on the number of symbols or squares of which a machine could be "directly aware." This reflects the fact that humans can observe only a certain number of symbols at one moment. If we want to observe more we have to use successive observations. In the simplest case, we observe one symbol at a time, and it is for this reason that Turing constrained his machines to be "directly aware" of only a single square of the tape at a time. Nothing fundamental is lost by doing this, it simplifies the analysis, and it further reflects the fact that humans working with paper and pencil almost invariably write only one symbol at a time.

Fourth, Turing specified a bound on what he called "changes of distribution of observed squares." The point of this constraint is to reflect the fact that there are physical limits on human shifts of attention. If I am attending to the computer screen on my desk at home, I cannot immediately shift my attention to the computer screen on my desk at work that is 4 miles away. My perceptions and actions are bounded by constraints of place, and it is this that Turing's fourth constraint reflects. He implemented it by specifying that his machines could move only one square at a time. Again, nothing fundamental is lost by doing this.

It should be clear from the previous that far from being an arbitrary construction, the Turing machine was carefully designed to reflect the constraints on human algorists and their interactions with their environments. The Turing machine is, it is true, a model of a very narrow slice of general human competence, but that is not the issue of immediate concern. The immediate issue is its plausibility as a formal model of a human algorist. Let me finally briefly address the points about reliability and speed made by Shaw and McIntyre. It is true that Turing machines are assumed to be perfectly reliable and to work as fast as one wishes, but neither point invalidates the Turing machine as a satisfactory model of the algorist. Turing machines incorporate the fundamental principles of effective calculation, whereas reliability and speed are adventitious practical considerations. They are important but separable from the theoretical requirements. Turing's analysis addresses the question of the conditions that enable a human to carry out a calculation effectively. One of those conditions is the ability to read and write symbols reliably. The analysis does not rule out an account of the conditions that might interfere with effective calculation, but that was not part of Turing's purpose. Reliability and speed are performance constraints rather than competence constraints.

VON NEUMANN'S CONJECTURE

Turing's (1936) analysis provided an account of the process of computation that includes elements modeling the algorist and elements modeling the environment. It is generally accepted as the most natural formalization of the intuitive notion of an effective procedure for calculation and, as the previous section shows, it respects the constraints on human algorists. The question remains whether Turing's analysis can form the foundation for a more general theory of automata or whether that path is blocked by Von Neumann's (1966) conjecture, as Shaw suggests. This aspect of the Shavian critique has had its most recent statement in Shaw (2003). In that article Shaw listed a number of theses or claims that he attributed to Herbert Simon's work on the study of artificial systems. One of these is the claim that complex systems can be reduced to simpler form by proper description. Shaw argued that some ideas of the mathematician John Von Neumann can be used to make an alternative case that asserts that "for systems beyond a certain level of finite complexity, no verbal description or mathematical formulation can reduce its [sic] complexity" (Shaw, 2003, p. 61). Shaw goes on to say that Von Neumann's work may justify "an even more pessimistic conjecture" (p. 61). It is not entirely straightforward to state this more pessimistic conjecture precisely but, roughly speaking, it amounts to the assertion that the question "What can this object do?" is of a higher logical type than the question "What is the structure of this object?" The difference this makes is that it can take infinitely longer to answer higher type questions about behavior.

Shaw made a more detailed analysis of the conjecture many years ago in an article that was originally published in 1971 before the algorist article was written and later republished (Shaw, 1976). In that article, he distinguished strong and weak versions of the conjecture that he described as "fundamentally different." The strong interpretation maintains that

> a formal understanding of truly complex natural phenomena is inaccessible to us due to the logical impossibility of codifying significant properties of complex systems in terms of simpler systems of abstract principles (e.g., a model). (p. 162)

The weak interpretation, which Shaw suggested was "more in keeping with Von Neumann's intent," asserts that

> some (but not necessarily all) approaches to modeling are inherently inadequate for providing explanations of complex phenomena which pass muster under the criterion of conceptual economy, although the same approaches may be quite adequate when directed toward explaining simple to moderately complex phenomena. (p. 162)

Shaw's view in 1976 was that the strong interpretation of the conjecture might foster a cynical attitude toward psychology, was unwise on pragmatic grounds, and was not forced on us on logical grounds. He appears to have hardened his view somewhat since then and now leans more toward the strong version of the conjecture because in Shaw (2003) he cited the work of Penrose (1989, 1994) and Rosen (1991, 2000), both of whom, in somewhat different ways, argued that "living systems are complex exactly because they exhibit behaviors not algorithmically computable" (Shaw, 2003, p. 63).

Several of von Neumann's works are relevant to questions about the study of complex systems and the development of a theory of complex automata. It is quite clear that von Neumann thought a properly founded theory would be applicable to both natural and artificial systems. He did not make the distinction between theories of living systems and theories of artifacts that Rosen (1991, 2000) treated as fundamental. The discussion here draws on three of Von Neumann's works: the paper he read at the Hixon symposium in Pasadena, California in September 1948, which is reprinted in Aspray and Burks (1987); a series of five lectures given at the University of Illinois in December 1949 that were published posthumously (Von Neumann, 1966)—this is the main source used by Shaw in his discussions of Von Neumann; finally, a short book that made comparisons between computers and brains, also published posthumously (Von Neumann, 1958). The book was started in 1955 and was unfinished when Von Neumann died in 1957. The chronology is of importance in reaching conclusions about how best to interpret some difficult aspects of Von Neumann's thought.

In the Hixon symposium paper (Aspray & Burks, 1987), as in the other works discussed here, Von Neumann's primary concern was to sketch an outline for a theory of complex automata. He said that

> a detailed, highly mathematical, and more specifically analytical, theory of automata and of information is needed. We possess only the first indications of such a theory at present. In assessing artificial automata ... of only moderate size, it has been possible to get along in a rough, empirical manner without such a theory. There is every reason to believe that this will not be possible with more elaborate automata. (pp. 407–408)

The problem, he suggested, was that existing logical methods would lead to theoretical statements that were simpler than their objects, as theoretical statements must be if they are to be of any use, only when those objects were of modest complexity. With a highly complex object like a human brain or a very large computer, he thought that "any attempt to describe it by the usual literary or formal–logical method may lead to something less manageable and more involved." (p. 414). He went on to suggest that this view was buttressed by some results in "modern logic." These results are discussed in due course.

The fundamental reason why a complex automaton might prove resistant to simplification via existing logical methods lay, Von Neumann thought, in the relationship between structure and function that was different for simple and complex systems. It was, he said, the mark of a simple automaton that its behavior was of "a lower degree of complication than the automaton itself" (Aspray & Burks, 1987, p. 415). By contrast, it was possible for a complex automaton to exhibit functioning of a higher degree of complexity than its own structure. Von Neumann said that organisms are clear examples of automata that are complex in this way because their capacity for reproduction is a form of behavior that produces systems of equal or greater complexity.

To illuminate the discussion, Von Neumann drew attention to the work of McCulloch and Pitts (1943), who proved the equivalence of logical formulae and finite networks of idealized neurons. The equivalence proof shows that every description of a system in terms of logical formulae can, in principle, be translated into a neural network description and vice versa. However, the equivalence proof did not demonstrate that logical and network descriptions would be equally perspicuous. Von Neumann suggested that in simple cases the logical description of a system would simplify the network description but that in complex cases the reverse might be true. Taking as an example the visual brain, whose fundamental activity he thought to be the making of analogies, he argued that "it is perfectly possible that the simplest and only practical way to say what constitutes a visual analogy consists in giving a description of the connections of the visual brain" (Aspray & Burks, 1987, p. 414). The conclusion of the Hixon symposium paper was that logic might have to change to rise to the challenge of developing a theory of complex systems. Von Neumann did not suggest that logical methods were intrinsically unsuitable for the study of complex systems. He said a

> new, essentially logical, theory is called for in order to understand high-complication automata and, in particular, the central nervous system. It may be, however, that in this process logic will have to undergo a pseudomorphosis to neurology to a much greater extent than the reverse. (Aspray & Burks, 1987, p. 414)

The discussion of the Hixon symposium paper was sharpened and clarified in the Illinois lectures. The assertion that a description of the brain might be the simplest way to approach the complex concept of visual analogy was stated with striking force: "It is absolutely not clear a priori that there is any simpler description of what constitutes a visual analogy than a description of the visual brain" (Von Neumann, 1966, p. 47). The connection of this point with the results in logic mentioned previously was made more explicit. Von Neumann introduced the connection by reiterating the concept of an inverse relationship between structural and functional descriptions for simple and complex automata.

> There is a good deal in formal logics to indicate that the description of the functions of an automaton is simpler than the automaton itself, as long as the automaton is not very complicated, but that when you get to high complications, the actual object is simpler than the literary description. (p. 47)

He went on to say that the logical work he had in mind was a theorem of Gödel's that showed, as he put it, that "the description of an object, is one class type higher than the object and is therefore asymptotically [?][1] infinitely longer to describe." (p.47). A few pages later he made some further remarks that bear on the issue but that make a slightly different point. The further remarks begin with a brief discussion of the significance of Turing's proof of the unsolvability of the halting problem for Turing machines. Turing had shown that although there was a single machine, the universal machine that could simulate the processing of any other Turing machine by interpreting a symbolic description of it, there was no single machine that could tell from the description of a given machine whether it would halt or would continue its processing indefinitely. Using Turing's own terminology, his proof showed that there was no single general method to distinguish circular from circle-free machines. Von Neumann said Turing's proof showed that "you can build an organ which can do anything that can be done, but you cannot build an organ

---

[1] The brackets and question mark indicate that the transcript of the lectures from which von Neumann (1966) was put together was incomplete or incomprehensible at this point. The conclusions one can safely draw about Von Neumann's intended meaning must, therefore, be considered tentative, and it is important to try to find an interpretation that is consistent with other points he made.

which tells you whether it can be done" (p. 51). He then related Turing's proof to the theory of types, to Gödel's work and to his earlier remarks.

> It is connected with the theory of types and with the results of Gödel. The feature is just this, that you can perform within the logical type that's involved everything that's feasible, but the question of whether something is feasible in a type belongs to a higher logical type … in the complicated parts of formal logic it is always one order of magnitude harder to tell what an object can do than to produce the object. The domain of the validity of the question is of a higher type than the question itself. (p. 51)

Shaw (1976, p. 156; 2003, p. 61) took this passage to be the key to Von Neumann's conjecture, and I think he is right to do so. The difficulty, as Shaw himself has said, is to come to a clear understanding of exactly what Von Neumann meant and what the logical results imply for psychology. In the earlier of the two articles, in which he discussed the topic in detail, Shaw suggested that Von Neumann's intended meaning is clarified by a passage in one of the later Illinois lectures in which he discussed a specific kind of complexity. "It is effectivity in complication, or the potentiality to do things. I am not thinking about how involved the object is, but how involved its purposive operations are. In this sense, an object is of the highest degree of complexity if it can do very difficult and involved things" (Von Neumann, 1966, p. 78). Notice again here the distinction between structural issues (how involved the object is) and functional issues (how involved its purposive operations are).

In his later article, Shaw (2003) took a somewhat different line and related the conjecture directly to the theorem of Gödel, also proved by Tarski, that Von Neumann mentioned. But Shaw went further than this and aligned Von Neumann's thinking with the arguments of Penrose (1989, 1994) and Rosen (1991, 2000), to the effect that "living systems are complex exactly because they exhibit behaviors not algorithmically computable" (Shaw, 2003, p. 63). Later in the article, he asks the question "What if complexity is by nature rather than artifice (formal description) a limitless source of generatively specified impredicativities, that is, undecidable predicates, as Von Neumann, Penrose, and Rosen all suspected? What then?" (p. 98). This pregnant question is left unanswered, but Shaw's later conclusion is that "some radical, ecological version of science must replace the mechanistic science most psychologists adopt uncritically" (p. 101).

Let us recall at this point Von Neumann's (Aspray Burks, 1987) conclusion in the Hixon symposium paper, which was not that logical methods were unsatisfactory for the study of complex automata, as Shaw's analysis suggests, but that logic would need to become more like neurology. It is, of course, possible that Von Neumann had changed his mind by the time the Illinois lectures were prepared, but his short book on computers and brains, which was written later still, suggests otherwise. At the end of that book, Von Neumann made some remarks that supported the idea that his vision of automata theory involved a transformation of logic rather than its abandonment.

> Just as languages like Greek or Sanskrit are historical facts and not absolute logical necessities, it is only reasonable to assume that logics and mathematics are similarly historical, accidental forms of expression. They may have essential variants, i.e. they may exist in other forms than the ones to which we are accustomed. Indeed, the nature of the central nervous system and of the message systems that it transmits indicate positively that this is so ... the outward forms of *our* mathematics are not absolutely relevant from the point of view of evaluating what the mathematical or logical language *truly* used by the central nervous system is. (Von Neumann, 1958, pp. 81–82)

Given Von Neumann's continued emphasis on the logical language used by the central nervous system, it seems that Shaw's view of the conjecture in 1976 was probably closer to Von Neumann's intended meaning than the somewhat stronger view of Shaw (2003). I shall argue that Von Neumann's work does not indicate the need for a noncomputational theory. Moreover, although I shall not develop the arguments here, I think it can be shown that neither Penrose (1989, 1994) nor Rosen (1991, 2000) made a conclusive case against the use of computational methods in ecological psychology. Once again, though, although I come to different conclusions about the implications of Von Neumann's work, I am indebted to Shaw's instinct for the fundamental questions. I am not aware of any other psychological theorist who saw so early the significance of the issues concerning complexity that Von Neumann's work invites us to consider.

AN ALTERNATIVE INTERPRETATION
OF VON NEUMANN'S CONJECTURE

I shall offer an interpretation of von Neumann's writings that takes a much more optimistic view than Shaw (2003) of the possibilities for computational methods in psychology. Computing has illuminated many areas of psychology and biology as well as mathematics. It is noteworthy, for example, that computational methods have been of great importance in facilitating the study of nonlinear dynamical systems that authors such as Port and van Gelder (1995) have proposed as a replacement for computational thinking in psychology. Thompson and Stewart (1986), for example, in their textbook on nonlinear dynamics and chaos remarked on "a spectacular blossoming of nonlinear dynamics, made possible ... by the wide availability of powerful digital and analogue computers" (p. ix). This casts doubt on the idea that nonlinear dynamical systems thinking will replace computational methods.

The starting point for the alternative understanding of Von Neumann's conjecture is, once again, the theorem of Gödel that Von Neumann mentioned in the Illinois lectures. Arthur Burks, the editor of Von Neumann's manuscript, was puzzled by the reference because he was not aware of a theorem that had the characteristics described by Von Neumann, that is, a proof that the functional description of an automaton might be infinitely longer than its structural description and require a higher type of logical construct. Burks wrote to Gödel to ask if he could clarify the matter. His letter and Gödel's reply are both reported in Von Neumann (1966). Gödel's reply was characteristically careful and suggested that the reference might have been to his proof that a complete description of a formal language A cannot be given in A because the concept of truth of sentences of A cannot be defined in A. However, he warned that this might not have been the answer because higher logical types do not necessarily involve longer symbolic descriptions. He proposed that "what Von Neumann perhaps had in mind appears more clearly from the universal Turing machine" (Von Neumann, 1966, p. 56).

To understand the significance of Gödel's remarks it is essential to have in mind the fact that the behavior of a universal machine is determined by the description of the machine on its tape. If the description of the machine is changed, the behavior of the universal machine also changes. The point Gödel made about the universal machine was that because there was no decision procedure to predict its behavior, a complete description could only be given by enumerating all its instances. That would be an infinitely long task because a universal machine can simulate the processing of a countable infinity of Turing machines. The structural description of a universal machine is finite, however, because, like every other Turing machine, it has a finite machine table. For this reason Gödel said "the universal Turing machine, where the ratio of the two complexities is infinity, might then be considered to be a limiting case of other finite mechanisms. This immediately leads to Von Neumann's conjecture" (Von Neumann, 1966, p. 56).

The statement that "the ratio of the two complexities is infinity" links structural and behavioral issues. The two complexities are the structural and behavioral descriptions of a universal machine. The ratio is infinity because a complete description of the behavior of a universal machine is infinite, whereas a complete description of the structure of its control automaton is finite. This leads to Von Neumann's conjecture, as Gödel said, but does so in a way that is consistent with the possibility that every complex system is a mechanism. It does not show that complex systems exhibit uncomputable behaviors. A universal machine is complex by Von Neumann's definition but does not, of course, do anything uncomputable.[2]

Gödel's point about the ratio of infinities stems from the fact that the behavior of a universal machine has to be studied by enumerating its instances because there is no decision procedure to predict its behavior. Shaw takes the existence of

---

[2] Rosen (1991, 2000) treats complexity in a way that makes a universal machine simple by definition. Complex systems, in his terminology, are defined to be those that exhibit uncomputable behavior.

undecidable predicates to support the case for a nonmechanistic psychology. However, the existence of undecidable predicates does not undermine the claim that mechanistic explanation is an appropriate goal for psychology. The starting point for an explanation of this somewhat counterintuitive fact is the simple but important distinction between an individual Turing machine and the countably infinite set of all Turing machines. Proofs such as the unsolvability of the halting problem, which is a famous instance of undecidability, concern what finite methods can demonstrate about the set as a whole. This is quite distinct from what can be said about individual members of the set. The halting problem arises with respect to the distinction (mentioned earlier) that Turing made between machines that keep printing zeroes and ones ad infinitum, which he called "circle-free" machines, and those that print only a finite number of zeroes and ones, which he called "circular" machines. The problem can be posed as a question: Is there a general method that can be used to determine, in a finite number of steps, whether an arbitrary Turing machine is circular or circle-free? The proof that the problem is unsolvable shows that the answer to the question is "No." This is what it means to say that the predicates "circular" and "circle-free" are undecidable. The crucial instance on which the proof is based involves self-reference, and this feature is characteristic of other limitative results in logic such as Gödel's famous incompleteness theorem.

The general fact of undecidability does not show that the predicate in question is undecidable for every Turing machine, nor does it show that there must be machines for which it is undecidable. What it shows is just that there is no single method that can be applied to decide the question in every possible instance. Some instances, for example, self-referential ones, will require different methods, and it is this that leads to the requirement for the enumeration of instances. An example of an everyday predicate that is undecidable in general but has clearly decidable instances is the predicate "prints zero." Turing was able to prove that this predicate is undecidable because its decidability would imply that the halting problem could be solved. However, there are many machines for which the predicate "prints zero" is decidable. Any machine that does not have an instruction to print zero in its description is a decidable instance, as is any machine that can be shown to print zero after a finite number of steps.

How then, should we understand Von Neumann's conjecture in relation to psychology? If humans are complex for the same sorts of reasons as universal machines, their behavior will give rise to undecidable predicates that show that no single finite method of psychological enquiry can be specified in advance to give correct answers to all psychological questions. Psychology cannot, therefore, be a purely theoretical science. It has inescapable empirical or observational content. There are behaviors that are not entirely predictable in advance and can be understood only by observation or experiment. Few psychologists will be surprised by this result. Of more interest for ecological psychology, perhaps, Von Neumann's conjecture also suggests that the structural descriptions of complex systems, although they do not fully explain their behavior, are a useful and important source of information about them. In the case of humans this can be interpreted to mean that the study of the structure of the nervous system is an important source of psychological information.

BACK TO THE WHAT, THE HOW, AND THE WHO

The alternative interpretation of Von Neumann's (1966) conjecture, taken in conjunction with the understanding that Turing's (1936) analysis of computation does give an appropriate account of the algorist, has some natural and pleasing consequences for ecological psychology. These can be set in the context of Shaw and McIntyre's (1974) what, how, and who questions.

Starting with the who question, Turing's (1936) analysis described the algorist abstractly, in terms of a finite set of functional states that are related to each other and to the states of the environment. The structure of this system of states and the types of behavior in which it can engage are finitely specified, but its actual behavior, understood as a sequence of interactions with the environment, may be indefinitely long. Turing's analysis suggested, and later theorists proved, that the isolated algorist—that is, a finite automaton—is computationally less powerful than a Turing machine that has access to an unbounded environment. It is, therefore, a key postulate of Turing's theory that the behavioral complexity of the algorist is a function not just of its internal states but also of the use it makes of its environment. Turing's algorist, in other words, is essentially situated.

The answer to the question "What does the algorist do?" is that the algorist perceives a constrained portion of the environment and acts on it. Each perception–action cycle changes the algorist, the environment, or both and leads without a break to the next cycle. Although the algorist and the environment are distinct entities they are not separable as far as the analysis of behavior is concerned. Von Neumann's conjecture suggested that behavior may be indefinitely extended and thus that it cannot be predicted fully in advance. That is the conclusion to draw from Turing's proof of the unsolvability of the halting problem. It does not imply that any specific, situated instance of behavior is uncomputable.

The potentially infinite extent of the what of behavior fits well with observations that Gibson made repeatedly about what the environment affords the perceiver. In his statement of the theory of information pickup in *The Senses Considered as Perceptual Systems*, Gibson (1966) said "The environment provides an inexhaustible reservoir of information. Some men spend most of their lives looking, others listening, and a few connoisseurs spend their time in smelling, tasting, or touching. They never come to an end" (p. 269). In his later statement of the theory in *The Ecological Approach to Visual Perception* (Gibson, 1979/1986), he said "the information in ambient light, along with sound, odor, touches, and natural chemicals, is inexhaustible. A perceiver can keep on noticing facts about the world she lives in to the end of her life without ever reaching a limit" (p. 243).

The general answer to the how question is that knowledge is obtained from ongoing cycles of interaction between the algorist and the environment. Von Neumann's conjecture suggested that an important part of the answer to the how question is to be found in investigations of the logical functioning of the nervous system. This aspect of ecological psychology is least well developed at present. Turing's work provided only the barest outline of how to proceed. There are two reasons for this: the first is that Turing's immediate concern was with only a small part of the behavioral capability of the situated agent, namely the capacity to calculate. The second is that Turing's analysis of this limited capacity was purely abstract and functional.

Von Neumann discussed the issues involved in studying the nervous system in his Hixon symposium paper (Aspray & Burks, 1987). The problem, he thought, was to account for what he called "general syndromes" of behavior as opposed to "special phases." A special phase of behavior is, for example, something like the capacity to treat two objects as instances of the class "triangle." Von Neumann thought that any special phase could be described exhaustively and that it would be a form of "logical mysticism" to deny it, but he qualified this assertion in the following important way. "It is, however, an important limitation, that this applies only to every element separately, and it is far from clear how it will apply to the entire syndrome of behavior." (Aspray & Burks, 1987, p. 413). The point he was making was further elucidated in the discussion following the paper. In response to a question he said,

> The problem, then is not this: How does the central nervous system effect any one, particular thing? It is rather: How does it do all the things that it can do, in their full complexity? What are the principles of its organization? How does it avoid really serious, that is, lethal, malfunctions over periods that seem to average many decades? (p. 424)

Von Neumann seemed to be making two slightly different points. One is that it may be a very complicated matter to describe everything the nervous system can do because it has such a wide range of capabilities. Thus its behavioral description may be indefinitely long. This is the case for a universal machine as Gödel indicated. However, there is a second point that is that it is a complex problem to understand how the nervous system is organized so as to support the error-free functioning of so many different capabilities. Von Neumann did not specifically mention the fact that the human agent is a complex system in which multiple activities proceed simultaneously, but the obvious challenge that this behavioral virtuosity presents to the psychological theorist is implicit in what he says.

Gibson's concept of a perceptual system is relevant to questions about the multiple activities that human agents engage in simultaneously and may be interpreted as the foundation for a theory of the relations between "special phases" of behavior and "general syndromes." The senses may be thought of as instances of special phases of behavior, whereas perceptual systems are instances of general syndromes that coordinate the activities of the senses. Support for this view can be found in Gibson (1966):

> When the "senses" are considered as active systems they are classified by modes of activity not by modes of conscious quality. ... Some of the systems, moreover, will pick up the same information as others, redundant information, while some will not, and they will cooperate in varying combinations. (p. 49)

The study of specific affordances elucidates the individual things that agents can do but leaves untouched the general question of how it is that agents can reliably perceive, select among, and act on the countless affordances that human environments offer. This question can also be tackled within a theory of perceptual systems or general syndromes of behavior.

The fact that agents sometimes misperceive the affordances of the environment or fall prey to illusions is another aspect of complexity. Gibson (1979/1986) was, of course, aware of the significance of errors in the study of perception. He was clear that "a concept of information is required that admits of the possibility of illusion. Illusions are a theoretical perplexity in any approach to the study of perception" (p. 243).

Von Neumann's suggestion that the structure of the patterns of connectivity in the visual brain might be the best way to understand the complexities of visual processing may be slow to achieve acclaim among ecological psychologists but does, nevertheless, point in a fruitful direction. When seen in the light of Turing's (1936) ecological analysis of the relation between the algorist and the environment the functional study of the nervous system supports rather than threatens ecological analysis. The converse is also true and may help to explain why some neuroscientists, for example Nakayama (1994), have found Gibson's approach important for their work.

Turing's analysis left the question about general syndromes of behavior unanswered because the computation of numbers is clearly a "special phase." Traditional computational theory of mind uses the universal machine concept to answer the general question via the notions of simulation and internal representation, but that is not a plausible solution for a range of reasons that have been discussed in the ecological literature. What we need to understand is how the functional states that model the algorist in the performance of one particular task are related to those that model the performance of another task. It was to answer this question that Von Neumann thought logic needed to undergo a change and become more probabilistic and neurological. The statistical character of contemporary neural network theory suggests that logic has indeed progressed in that direction. However, there are also developments in the area of concurrency theory that suggest the continued value of discrete state methods. In particular, process algebras such as the π-calculus (Milner, 1999; Sangiorgi & Walker, 2001) that have been developed to study systems of interacting nondeterministic processes may prove suitable for the study of interacting functions generally. This kind of study may make a significant contribution to the kind of theory that Von Neumann thought was needed for an understanding of general syndromes of behavior and that Gibson was arguing for with the concept of a perceptual system.

CONCLUSIONS

Turing's analysis of computation provided a rigorous model of the situated algorist that specifically takes account of the constraints under which real agents function. It provides a formal answer to the who question that Shaw and McIntyre (1974) placed at the heart of their vision of psychology. Turing's proof of the unsolvability of the halting problem demonstrates that the what question cannot be answered a priori with full generality. There is no single process that can tell, from the structural description of a system alone, exactly how that system will behave. To understand a system fully one must study it as its behavior unfolds. This form of knowledge is different from the knowledge that can be acquired by studying the structure of the system, but both forms are needed. Turing's analysis does not provide a full answer to the how question because it abstracts from the details of systems under study and characterizes them in terms of functional states. Von Neumann indicated that an adequate theory of complex automata would still be logical in character but that our understanding of logic would most likely be transformed into something more probabilistic and neurological.

The theoretical significance of the algorist has been clear to ecological psychologists since Shaw and McIntyre discussed the issue in 1974. The theoretical significance of Von Neumann's conjecture is more difficult to gauge immediately but may prove equally important in the long term. Shaw has done a service to ecological psychology and to the broader psychological community by being the first to explore in detail some of the ramifications of Von Neumann's complex thinking about complexity. It is appropriate that the last words, with whose sentiments I thoroughly agree, should come from Shaw: "The positive import derived from a serious consideration of Von Neumann's conjecture leads us then to reopen some old doors and admonishes us to peer more deeply into the nature of complexity" (1976, p. 167).

ACKNOWLEDGMENTS

I would like to thank Claudia Carello for inviting me to take part in the Festschrift in honor of Bob Shaw, for which this article was written. I would also like to thank Claudia Carello and Michael Turvey, Bob and Dot Shaw, and Claire Michaels and

Jean Haskell for their hospitality during my visit. Bill Mace cut short a sunny Sunday afternoon by the pool to drive me to the airport, for which kindness I am very grateful.

REFERENCES

Aspray, W., & Burks, A. (Eds.). (1987). *Papers of John von Neumann on computing and computer theory: Vol. 12 in the Charles Babbage Institute reprint series for the history of computing.* Cambridge, MA: MIT Press.

Church, A. (1936). An unsolvable problem of elementary number theory. *American Journal of Mathematics, 58,* 345–363.

Eberbach, E., Goldin, D., & Wegner, P. (2004). Turing's ideas and models of computation. In C. Teuscher (Ed.), *Alan Turing: Life and legacy of a great thinker* (pp. 159–194). Berlin, Germany: Springer-Verlag.

Gandy, R. O., & Yates, C. E. M. (Eds.). (2001). *Collected works of A. M. Turing. Mathematical logic.* Amsterdam: Elsevier.

Gibson, J. J. (1966). *The senses considered as perceptual systems.* Boston : Houghton Mifflin.

Gibson, J. J. (1986). *The ecological approach to visual perception.* Hillsdale, NJ: Lawrence Erlbaum Associates, Inc. (Original work published 1979)

Harnad, S. (Ed.). (1987). *Categorical perception. The groundwork of cognition.* Cambridge, England: Cambridge University Press.

Jaffrey, M. (1995). *Madhur Jaffrey's illustrated Indian cookery.* London: BBC Books.

Kleene, S. C. (1936). λ-definability and recursiveness. *Duke Mathematical Journal, 2,* 340–353.

McCulloch, W. S., & Pitts, W. (1943). A logical calculus of the ideas immanent in nervous activity. *Bulletin of Mathematical Biophysics, 5,* 115–133.

Milner, R. (1999). *Communicating and mobile systems: The π-calculus.* Cambridge, England: Cambridge University Press.

Nakayama, K. (1994). James J. Gibson—An appreciation. *Psychological Review, 101*(2), 329–335.

Penrose, R. (1989). *The emperor's new mind. Concerning computers, minds, and the laws of physics.* New York: Oxford University Press.

Penrose, R. (1994). *Shadows of the mind. A search for the missing science of consciousness.* New York: Oxford University Press.

Port, R. F., & van Gelder, T. (Eds.). (1995). *Mind as motion. Explorations in the dynamics of cognition.* Cambridge, MA: MIT Press.

Rosen, R. (1991). *Life itself. A comprehensive inquiry into the nature, origin, and fabrication of life.* New York: Columbia University Press.

Rosen, R. (2000). *Essays on life itself.* New York: Columbia University Press.

Sangiorgi, D., & Walker, D. (2001). *The p-calculus. A theory of mobile processes.* Cambridge, England: Cambridge University Press.

Shaw, R. E. (1976). Cognition, simulation, and the problem of complexity. In J. M. Scandura (Ed.), *Structural learning II. Issues and approaches* (pp. 153–167). New York: Gordon & Breach.

Shaw, R. E. (2003). The agent–environment interface: Simon's indirect or Gibson's direct coupling? *Ecological Psychology, 15,* 37–106.

Shaw, R. E., & McIntyre, M. (1974). Algoristic foundations to cognitive psychology. In W. B. Weimer & D. S. Palermo (Eds.), *Cognition and the symbolic processes* (pp. 305–362). Hillsdale, NJ: Lawrence Erlbaum Associates, Inc.

Siegelmann, H. T. (1999). *Neural networks and analog computation. Beyond the Turing limit.* New York: Birkhäuser Boston.

Stannett, M. (2004). Hypercomputational models. In C. Teuscher (Ed.), *Alan Turing: Life and legacy of a great thinker* (pp. 135–157). Berlin: Springer-Verlag.

Thompson, J. M. T., & Stewart, H. B. (1986). *Nonlinear dynamics and chaos. Geometrical methods for engineers and scientists*. Chichester, England: Wiley.

Turing, A. M. (1936). On computable numbers, with an application to the entscheidungsproblem. *Proceedings of the London Mathematical Society, Series. 2, 42,* 230–265.

Turing, A. M. (1950) Computing machinery and intelligence. *Mind, 59,* 433–460.

Von Neumann, J. (1958). *The computer and the brain*. New Haven, CT: Yale University Press.

Von Neumann, J. (1966). *Theory of self-reproducing automata*. Urbana: University of Illinois Press.

Wells, A. J. (2002). Gibson's affordances and Turing's theory of computation. *Ecological Psychology, 14,* 141–180.

Wells, A. J. (2004). Cognitive science and the Turing machine: An ecological perspective. In C. Teuscher (Ed.), *Alan Turing: Life and legacy of a great thinker* (pp. 271–292). Berlin: Springer-Verlag.

ECOLOGICAL PSYCHOLOGY, 17(3 & 4), 231–232

Article Index for
Ecological Psychology
Volume 17 (2005)

NUMBERS 3&4

SPECIAL ISSUE:
SYMMETRY AND DUALITY:
PRINCIPLES FOR AN ECOLOGICAL PSYCHOLOGY, I

ECOLOGICAL PSYCHOLOGY, 17(3 & 4), 233–234
Copyright © 2005, Lawrence Erlbaum Associates, Inc.

Author Index for
Ecological Psychology
Volume 17 (2005)

For Product Safety Concerns and Information please contact our EU representative GPSR@taylorandfrancis.com Taylor & Francis Verlag GmbH, Kaufingerstraße 24, 80331 München, Germany

T - #0155 - 270225 - C0 - 229/152/6 - PB - 9780805894073 - Gloss Lamination